PICTURING RHODE ISLAND
Images of Everyday Life 1850–2006

PICTURING RHODE ISLAND
Images of Everyday Life 1850–2006

MAUREEN A. TAYLOR

Commonwealth Editions
Beverly, Massachusetts

To George P. White (1916–1992), a man who knew history and liked to share it

Copyright © 2007 by Maureen A. Taylor
All rights reserved. No part of this book may be reproduced in any form or by any electronic or mechanical means without permission in writing from the publisher, except by a reviewer, who may quote brief passages in a review.

Library of Congress Cataloging-in-Publication Data
    Taylor, Maureen Alice.
    Picturing Rhode Island : images of everyday life, 1850-2006 / Maureen A. Taylor.
       p. cm.
    Includes index.
    ISBN 978-1-933212-39-5 (alk. paper)
        1. Rhode Island—History—Pictorial works. 2. Rhode Island—Pictorial works. I. Title.

F80.T395 2007
974.5—dc22
        2007005444

Cover design by John Barnett
Interior design by Anna L. Geraghty
Printed in China
Published by Commonwealth Editions
an imprint of Memoirs Unlimited, Inc.
266 Cabot Street, Beverly, Massachusetts 01915
www.commonwealtheditions.com

CONTENTS

Acknowledgments   *iv*

Introduction   *vi*

CHAPTER ONE	The March of Time: Providence	2
CHAPTER TWO	Our Architectural Heritage: Where We Live	22
CHAPTER THREE	Getting Around: On the Water, Traveling Roads, and Riding the Rails	42
CHAPTER FOUR	On the Bay: Recreation and Resorts	68
CHAPTER FIVE	Out on the Town: City Amusements	96
CHAPTER SIX	Industrial and Commercial Genius: Economic Success and Commercial Activity	116
CHAPTER SEVEN	Earning a Living: Making Ends Meet	136
CHAPTER EIGHT	Building Rhode Island: A Century of Change	160

Index   182

A week after the blizzard of 1978, I climbed over the snow banks in Providence's Hope Street for a job interview as an Assistant Graphics Curator at the Rhode Island Historical Society. The researchers I met and the staff I worked with over the years inspired me to write and share what I learned about Rhode Island, the history of photography, and genealogy. This is a book I've always wanted to write. Thank you, Webster Bull of Commonwealth Editions, for seeing this project as one worth publishing!

There are always plenty of people to thank for their help in the production of a book. This book is no different. Writing and researching this manuscript put me back in touch with librarians, archivists, and collectors I knew when I worked with the Rhode Island Historical Society.

Bill Connors, a teacher at LaSalle Academy in Providence and a collector of Rhode Island material, let me browse through his extensive collection of stereographs. Many thanks to Bill for providing these images.

Betty Fitzgerald, Rhode Island Collection librarian at the Providence Public Library, showed me the library's photo collection and helped me track down all the little details to date and identify each image I wanted to include. In addition, for

ACKNOWLEDGMENTS

several months I spent every Monday night working at the public library, and the reference staff were very helpful in retrieving books and maps for this endeavor.

Ken Carlson and Tracey Croce of the Rhode Island State Archives shared their knowledge of the photographs in their collection. Their exhibits are a must-see for those with an interest in Rhode Island history who find themselves walking by 337 Westminster Street, in downtown Providence.

Some contacts from my former life at the Rhode Island Historical Society resulted in a new discovery. Looking for previously unpublished photographs of Rhode Island, I called Sam Hough, a former Brown University librarian turned rare book dealer and now the proprietor of Owl at the Bridge. Sam gave me a tour of the Gorham Collection at the John Hay Library at Brown University. He also suggested I contact Larry DePetrillo, an avid collector of Rhode Island material. Some of the best construction photographs in this manuscript are from DePetrillo's collection.

A few years ago, Matthew Isenburg, a daguerreotype collector, mentioned that he had an early image of Providence. Thank you, Matthew, for letting me include it. It's the only daguerreotype in the book.

Susan Millard, a former Rhode Island Historical Society colleague who now works at the Pawtucket Public Library, provided assistance and advice on using that institution's local history collection.

At the Newport Historical Society, I kept the librarian, Bert Lippincott, and the photographic curator, Kim Krazer, busy for an entire day finding interesting images of Newport. Thank you to Bert for verifying all the little facts about Newport that I needed to write captions.

Thank you to the staff of the Providence Warwick Convention and Visitors Bureau, especially to Alissa Bateman, for making available current images of Providence.

Jane Schwerdtfeger, an educator, art historian, and steadfast friend, read every word and looked at each photograph. Thank you, Jane, for everything, especially for keeping me on the right track.

Al Klyberg, former director of the Rhode Island Historical Society, and William Mackenzie Woodward, of the Rhode Island Historic Preservation Commission, helped me get my facts straight. In the end, of course, any errors are mine.

How many photographs does it take to tell Rhode Island's story? There is no one answer. I looked at hundreds of pictures in archives, publications, and private collections to compile the images in this book. One curator was surprised that I was trying to cover the whole state in one volume. Rhode Island is a small state with a rich history and an extensive photographic record. It's not the number of photographs that tells a tale, it's the arrangement and quality of the images. Although not every community is included, I selected photographs that I thought gave an impression of the state as a whole. To illustrate the rate of change, in most chapters I included a collection of images showing a particular parcel of land over time. As with a photographic flipbook, you can focus on a notable landmark while the area around it undergoes a transformation.

I've worked with images of Rhode Island for decades. Some are so familiar I can close my eyes and see them clearly, but when a photograph becomes commonplace it's hard to see what is really happening in it, what it actually shows. We begin to take familiar images for granted. For this book I needed to find a way to view these pictures with a fresh eye. To accomplish this, it wasn't

INTRODUCTION

enough just to put them aside and pick them up later. Instead, I used photo editing software and scanners to enlarge the photographs to see their details. In some cases, the "new" elements were startling. In a familiar photo, an old shop turned out to contain a painting of Jack the Ripper, and the painted symbolism on the exterior pointed to its real purpose—as a pawn shop. In a much-published view of Market Square, a man on crutches suddenly became visible. Whole pigs wait for slaughter in front of stores, and people peer from windows watching events. Researching these details resulted in a better understanding of the history behind an image. Though there are always unanswered questions, I've done my best to fill in the gaps. Each caption explains what's in the picture and its significance.

The photographic history represented here covers more than a hundred and fifty years; the earliest image dates from the 1850s and the most recent from 2006.

These photographs were taken for a variety of purposes. Stereographs—images that appeared three-dimensional when viewed through a special device—were created to entertain our ancestors and give them a record of tourist sites. Photographers shot pictures as marketing tools for specific businesses. Some photographs are documents through which one can trace the progress of a construction project or find proof of child labor. A few are random shots by an interested cameraman. In many cases, the photographer remains anonymous.

As you look at these photographs closely, study them to see the differences between now and then. Take out a magnifying glass and really look at them. You'll see a man sharpening his knife to cut meat for a bonneted housewife, workmen laboring on a warm day with their coats draped beside them, and lots of children staring at the photographers who were snapping pictures. Every image offers you a glimpse into the everyday life, work, and play of Rhode Island and an opportunity to experience our state as an observer of the past.

Change happens unevenly. Certain neighborhoods stay the same for generations, but a single block can change drastically several times in a single lifetime. Tracing the history of a particular area in photographs allows us to see how rapidly things evolve around familiar landmarks. In downtown Providence, social and economic shifts caused a reshaping of whole city blocks. This process continues today with several new construction projects under way.

The city's original business district stretched along the Providence waterfront at the base of College Hill, with the Market House in the center. As commerce moved across the Providence River in the early nineteenth century, bridges provided access to the new enterprises in the earlier residential areas of Weybosset and Westminster streets. Also in this new downtown was a section of the city known as Exchange Place, the present-day Kennedy Plaza, an area currently defined by the placement of the Providence City Hall, the old Union Station, and the Federal Building. Even though the Civil War Monument, also called the Soldiers and Sailors Monument, was frequently repositioned in the plaza, it remains a recognizable landmark, but the cityscape around it in old photographs is barely recognizable today. The train station moved three times, from an area currently occupied by a small park across from the present bus-loading area to the filled-in land of

CHAPTER ONE

THE MARCH OF PROGRESS
Providence

the old Cove, a circular body of water created from one of the rivers running through the city. Now the trains arrive and leave from a station across from the State House. On the other side of Kennedy Plaza stands the Union Station complex; the old train station is now office space. Behind it is Waterplace Park (1988-1994), a component of the Capital Center Project, which revitalized part of Providence with a mall, hotels, new office complexes, and the addition of high-rise luxury condominiums.

Nearby is the corner of Washington Street, where in the mid-nineteenth century a salvage yard was located, followed by a commercial block in the late nineteenth century, and now home to the Biltmore Hotel. Further into the mercantile section of town is the corner of Dorrance and Weybosset streets. A four-story dwelling occupied that spot until 1878, when developers built the Narragansett Hotel. Now Johnson and Wales University, the culinary institute, owns the building at that junction that used to be WJAR's Broadcast House. Johnson and Wales, along with other Rhode Island academic institutions, transformed sections of the center city into an urban campus.

In this chapter, you take a tour of these changes. To orient yourself, watch for known landmarks such as streets, buildings, and statues.

SOLDIERS AND SAILORS MONUMENT, c. 1871

In this early photograph of the civic center of Providence, later named Exchange Place and, later still, Kennedy Plaza, a group stands in front of the newly dedicated Soldiers and Sailors Monument, later known simply as the Civil War Monument. The monument bears brass plates with the names of the dead, and brass figures commemorate the soldiers and sailors who fought. At this time, Exchange Place was a small area bounded by the shops seen behind the monument and on the other side by the train station. The couple with the small child in the center of the image is prominent in a scene that is otherwise populated mostly by men. Perhaps they are parents or siblings of a dead soldier.

BUTLER EXCHANGE, c. 1878, STEREOGRAPH BY LEANDER BAKER

The commercial side of cobblestone-paved Exchange Place, located behind the Civil War Monument, changed from a series of low buildings and small shops to multistory office structures by the mid- to late nineteenth century. A boy in a cap stands in front of the six-story Butler Exchange; at the time it was the largest building in Providence, extending from Exchange Place to Westminster Street. A street vendor sells food from a cart to the left of the entrance. First-floor occupants included Fowler Brothers and Fessenden (hats, caps, and men's furnishings), Brown Brothers & Company, and C. Farnum & Co. On the second floor, the Providence Public Library rented space for a brief period beginning in 1878. Photographer Leander Baker (c.1844–1925) produced many of the stereographs in this collection.

EXCHANGE PLACE, LOOKING WEST, c. 1873, STEREOGRAPH BY E. AND H. T. ANTHONY AND CO.

In the foreground are the Civil War Monument, on Exchange Place, and the intersection of Cove, Dorrance, and Washington streets. Behind the monument is Harrington's Opera House, originally named City Hall when it opened on January 4, 1865, because the owners leased the land from the city. In 1871 the theater became known as Harrington's. G. S. Hall's French and American Confectionary sold candy, cigars, and tobacco on the first floor of the building. On the corner is a triangular lot used by the abutting mills and machine shops for storage and refuse. In the center of the lot, a cart is being loaded. A high wooden fence covered with broadside posters hides the sight of piles of barrels and pipes from pedestrians' eyes. A lone man stands at the intersection.

CITY HALL AND EXCHANGE PLACE, FROM BUTLER EXCHANGE, c. 1885

The Butler Exchange in Exchange Place provides a good vantage point for a view, looking northwest, of the evolving landscape of downtown Providence. Harrington's is gone, replaced by the Providence City Hall. It took four years from the groundbreaking in 1874 to the dedication in 1878 for this Second Empire–style municipal building to be finished.

Carriages wait out front and on the side street to the left. A wide sidewalk and streetlights surround the Civil War Monument. To the right, the same decrepit triangular lot seen in an earlier view is visible adjacent to several small factories. Behind them are newer multistory mill structures. The high wooden fence is still there, capped by an advertisement for the Hotel Dorrance.

EXCHANGE PLACE, c. 1915

As a policeman directs automobile traffic, three men stroll across Exchange Place in front of the Butts Block Building. This triangular commercial block replaced the storage dump on the corner of Washington and Dorrance streets. Crowds line the sidewalks, waiting their turn to cross, while other pedestrians hurry through the busy intersection. Reiner's Druggist occupies the corner spot and advertises its presence with electric signs. Reiner's had two other locations: one downtown and one on the East Side. Other companies use rooftop billboards to advertise everything from California fruit to tires. A banner on the side announces that Central Auto Tires is forced to vacate the premises. An electric railway car, ready to travel along the route of the overhead cables, picks up passengers at Washington Street.

THE BILTMORE HOTEL, c. 1930

Trolleys and cars flow down Washington Street, past the Biltmore Hotel, built on the site of the Butts Block Building. The Providence Chamber of Commerce raised funds to build the Biltmore, which provided first-class accommodations to business travelers. It opened for business in 1922. Across the street in front of the building, people wait for public transportation beneath a shelter. Pedestrians walk along Exchange Place and on side streets in front of traffic. To the right, the Bryant and Stratton College sign can be seen.

EXCHANGE PLACE, c. 1873, STEREOGRAPH IN "THE AMERICAN SCENERY SERIES"

On the opposite side of the plaza from the City Hall, men lean on the railings overlooking the pilings being driven into place for the construction of the Central Fire Station. Covered wagons are parked at the curb facing the train station. Behind the depot, the tree-lined walkway surrounding the Cove can be seen. On the left, groups of men lay cobblestones for the roadway. In the center a horse drinks from a ground-level water trough. Created in 1846, the elliptical Cove, located behind the train station in Exchange Place, had public walkways and landscaped grounds. Tidal-flow issues and pollution contributed to the city's decision to fill in this body of water in the 1890s. This new land created space for a new train station and several new streets.

EXCHANGE PLACE, LOOKING EAST, c. 1887

The photographer stood in the center of Exchange Place to take this image of the statue of General Ambrose Burnside, a Union general in the Civil War, and the Central Fire Station, built in 1873. The statue was dedicated in 1887, and was moved to City Hall Park in 1906.

Canal Street Hose Company No. 1, Hook and Ladder Company No. 1, and Protective Company No. 1 shared space on the first floor of the two-story French-style fire house, leading to the station's nickname, the Three Ones. This Central Fire Station was demolished in 1902, after a new Central Fire House had been constructed.

In front of the fire station, a fireman polishes a piece of fire-fighting apparatus. In the center doorway a man sits in front of another piece of equipment. The dark blur coming toward the viewer is a person walking on a sidewalk too fast for the shutter to freeze the action.

EXCHANGE PLACE, 1883

An African American driver lets his horse drink from a water fountain in the center of the plaza. Nearby a flat bed freight wagon, known as a "low-boy," stands empty, waiting for a teamster. On the right is Union Passenger Depot with wagons and hacks lined up at the entrance, while an omnibus passes by. Farther down Exchange Place, City Hall and the Civil War Monument can be seen. On the left, the commercial district is busy with customers at businesses such as Jessop & Sons (iron and steel), the American Supply Company, and Lees Governor Company. A line of streetlights runs down the center of Exchange Place, illuminating the area at night. On the right, traffic traveling through the plaza creates a blur.

EXCHANGE PLACE, c. 1890

This elevated view, taken from the Washington Buildings in Washington Square, overlooks Exchange Place to the west. In the foreground is the Central Fire Station. Wagons and carriages line up in front of the twin-towered Union Passenger Depot. To the right a train sits on the tracks of the station. At this time while the Cove was being filled to create new land, the trees of the Cove Promenade Park were still in place behind the station. At the far end is the City Hall, which towers over the neighborhood behind it. Telephone wires strung across rooftops and poles crisscross the scenery.

UNION PASSENGER DEPOT, 1896

A fire destroyed the Union Passenger Depot on February 20, 1896. Here, onlookers bundled up against the cold view the ice-covered damage; near them is a horse-drawn sled. Pedestrians walk by the brick shell. At the time of the fire, a new railroad station was already being constructed on the area behind this building, once the site of the Cove. A temporary station was built to be used until the new passenger depot opened.

12   CONSTRUCTION OF BRIDGE OVER PROVIDENCE RIVER, c. 1904

Workers use a lever and pulley system to place steel girders for the construction of a bridge connecting Exchange Place to the East Side. This bridge became known as Post Office Bridge after the Federal Building, which contained a post office, opened nearby.

Office workers stand nearby to watch while men operate the cables. A single man stands in the pit, moving the supports into position. Behind this scene are the new Central Fire Station, which opened in 1903, and the elevated tracks of the railroad station.

FEDERAL BUILDING, EXCHANGE PLACE, c. 1925

The Federal Building was located next to the Central Fire Station at the east end of Exchange Place. Near the large entranceway on the right, a young boy in a uniform tends a car parked there. Automobiles park nose into the curb in the center traffic circle. A man walks down the street while ahead of him cars drive toward the East Side.

    The placement of this building shortened the length of the plaza to 900 feet, and the look of downtown changed with the addition of two streets, one on either side of the structure. After it opened in 1908, the area between it and Canal Street became known first as Post Office Square, after the post office in the building, and later Memorial Square.

14   UNION STATION, EXCHANGE PLACE, c. 1960

Built between 1896 and 1898, the five-building Union Station replaced the Union Passenger Depot, which burned down in 1896. In 1900 three hundred trains a day ran to and from this busy station. One of the five buildings was destroyed by fire in 1940, and another fire destroyed the interior in 1987. By that time the station had been replaced by the present station near the State House. The old Union Station now houses private offices.

    Here, a couple strolls hand in hand in hand while bus passengers wait on benches in front of the Union Station in Exchange Place. Cars travel underneath the elevated tracks into downtown. Banners from the New Haven Railroad announce an exhibit at the station, "Tomorrow's Train—Here Today," and the arrival of the Shrine Circus.

"SITE OF THE NARRAGANSETT HOTEL," PROVIDENCE, c. 1860

Within a couple of decades of this photo, this small hotel, located a short walk to the south of Exchange Place, was gone, replaced by a first-class business hotel, the Narragansett. A lone wagon waits in front of a shop on Dorrance Street, and around the corner on Broad Street a store selling harnesses has a display out front. At this time the area bounded by Broad (now Weybosset Street) and Dorrance streets was still a mix of commercial buildings and dwellings. Behind these structures are the Providence Steam and Gas Pipe Company on Pine Street and a furniture store.

NARRAGANSETT HOTEL, c. 1885, UNATTRIBUTED STEREOGRAPH

All the small shops and residential buildings, including the small brick hotel in the previous photo, were replaced in 1878 by the luxurious eight-story Narragansett Hotel. This million-dollar project had 225 rooms and entrances on Broad, Dorrance, and Eddy streets. Two hacks for hire wait for customers in front of the hotel. Awnings and signage on the first floor belong to retail establishments. The Narragansett Hotel closed in 1959 and was razed the next year. (The site was a parking lot until 1978–79, when the Outlet Communications Company built Broadcast House. That building is now owned by Johnson and Wales University.)

MARKET HOUSE, PROVIDENCE, c. 1865

Just as the Civil War Monument remained a constant in Exchange Place, the Market House, one of the earliest commercial buildings in the city, is a reference point for observing changes at the base of College Hill on the city's East Side. Market House was built in 1773 as a two-story central market on the site of the original town common, and a third floor was added in 1793 for use by the St. John's Masonic Lodge. On the first floor one could purchase meat, butter, poultry, and eggs; vegetables were sold from the basement. Customers passed through the central hall buying food from the stalls. Market House became the Providence City Hall from 1865 to 1878, until the completion of the new City Hall in Exchange Place.

After that, the Board of Trade (later the Providence Chamber of Commerce) occupied the building until the 1920s but the building remained vacant from the 1920s to World War II. In 1950, the city gave it to the Rhode Island School of Design.

Here, vendors and customers shield their eyes from the sun as, on the right side of the building, men in work smocks stand in front of the butcher shop identified by the cuts of meat on display. Notice the bull's horns attached to the front corner of the building. Under the display, a man in a top hat and a young man with a pair of crutches stand near the lamp post, next to a policeman. Across the street two men wait near an empty wagon.

**VIEW TOWARDS DOWNTOWN FROM
MARKET SQUARE, c. 1885
PHOTO BY THE HORTON BROTHERS**

A woman with packages and a couple of men stand on the corner of College Street, in the original commercial center of the city, on the East Side. In the distance are a horse-drawn trolley, a carriage, and the pedestrian traffic of Weybosset Street. Signs indicate that Market House, on the left, is home to the Board of Trade and various commodity brokers such as Randall, a cotton broker, and H. W. Angell's lumber. On the third floor a lawyer has his offices. On the right hand side of Market Square is the trolley depot for the Union Railway Company. Facing the square are the Union Bank and the Merchants National Bank. Behind the depot is Akerman's Blank Book Manufactory.

WASHINGTON BUILDINGS, VIEWED FROM MARKET HOUSE, c. 1910

The Providence Washington Insurance Company built the block-long Washington Buildings, where Akerman's factory had space, in 1843, and the structure stood until 1916. Twenty years after the previous view, looking toward downtown, one still sees people crossing the square, but the view has changed. The Union Railroad Depot has disappeared, torn down for bridge widening in 1897. "For Rent" and lease signs cover the windows of the Washington Buildings. The Reiner Co. is on the first floor.

MARKET SQUARE, c. 1896

This view of Market Square and the East Side was taken from the Banigan Building, a ten-and-a-half-story fireproof office building built by rubber producer Joseph Banigan in 1896. It's on the block bounded by Weybosset Street, Post Office Court, Dyer Street, and Exchange Street. On the left, the passenger depot has a line of trolleys in front. Market House is in the center of the photo. Across College Street, to the left of Market House, are the Hotel Bristol and the Atlantic Building. To the far right, a billboard for "Quaker Bitters" decorates the front of a commercial structure on Canal Street. Delivery wagons packed with goods are parked along the bridge.

MARKET SQUARE, c. 1920s

In this photo, Market House can be seen on the far right. Cars speed by using the Weybosset Street Bridge and the rotary in the middle of the bridge. A bus makes its way toward the East Side. To the left, across Weybosset Street, is the Merchants Bank Building, which was seen in an earlier view of Market Square. Towering over the downtown area, on the site where the Washington Buildings and two smaller structures once stood, is the eleven-story limestone Hospital Trust Building, which opened in 1919. Today, the library of the Rhode Island School of Design occupies the first floor.

WORLD WAR I MEMORIAL, c. 1946

Cars, trucks, taxis, and buses find their way through the rotary around Memorial Square and the World War I Memorial at the base of Steeple and Waterman streets. The earlier Post Office Square became Memorial Square when the monument was dedicated in 1929. For many years this area was affectionately known by local residents as Suicide Circle for its multiple converging lanes of traffic and chaotic travel patterns.

Behind the column, a Gilbane Co. cement truck backs into the construction scene. On the site of the former Gorham Manufacturing Company, a new building for the Providence Washington Insurance Company is under construction; it was finished in 1947. Behind that are the First Baptist Church and North Main Street. In the 1990s the seventy-five-foot granite monument was moved to a park in front of the Providence County Courthouse. The rotary is now gone.

PROVIDENCE SKYLINE, 2006

In the foreground, the old Union Station looks small compared to the skyscrapers in Kennedy Plaza, the old Exchange Place. The 1908 Federal Building is still here, as is the Industrial Bank Tower from 1928 with the Civil War Monument near its base. The Fleet Bank Building, with its stepped roof, is next to the newer Rhode Island Hospital Trust Bank building on the left. Since this photograph was taken, the skyline has changed again as new office complexes and high-rise luxury condos were under construction in 2006.

Rhode Island's architectural heritage was once visible in small towns as well as its larger cities. Many of the early residences were destroyed during the course of King Philip's War in 1675–76. Over the centuries, further destruction resulted from a combination of fires, neglect, and commercial progress. Some of the dwellings depicted in this chapter are preserved only in photographs. Others remain intact, converted to other purposes. A lucky few still house families.

Among the lost are seventeenth-century houses such as Henry Bull's Newport residence, Arthur Fenner's wood-frame house in Cranston, and the Jenks/Jenckes (variant spellings of the sur-

CHAPTER TWO

OUR ARCHITECTURAL HERITAGE
Where We Live

name) house in Pawtucket. The magnificent Tockwotton House, once home to the Reform School, and the City Hotel on Weybosset Street began as private residences whose size and location made them candidates for commercial development—but ultimately they were demolished and replaced by newer and larger structures. In Newport, the Matthews House burned more than a century ago. Dexter Asylum is also gone, but its stone walls still stand. Whole neighborhoods, like Providence's Constitution Hill, disappeared in the late twentieth century as a result of urban renewal programs.

Still-extant reminders of past lives are Newport's eighteenth-century Vernon House, now used as office space, and Hopelands, now part of the Rocky Hill School. Evidence of the immigrant influx to Rhode Island is present in late-nineteenth- and early-twentieth-century triple-decker houses.

This chapter focuses on where and how Rhode Islanders lived, from stone wall–enclosed farms to lighthouses to nineteenth-century mansions. The average houses of working families were dwarfed by the expansive real estate holdings of the rich. It's all here, depicted in photos of neighborhoods, cities, and notable historic properties.

VIEW FROM PROSPECT TERRACE, PROVIDENCE, EARLY 1870s

Two views from Prospect Terrace, a park on Providence's East Side with a panoramic view of the city, show this area of the city's transition from a residential community to a busy metropolis. The residents of this city ward presented Prospect Terrace to the city as a park in 1867. The first image predates the construction of a retaining wall and fence in 1877. The Roger Williams statue that overlooks the city dates from 1939.

In the foreground of the first photo, the spire of the First Baptist Church towers over the surrounding houses, while in the second it's barely visible to the right of Roger Williams's outstretched hand. On the far left of the older view is the tower of the Superior Court House (built 1877) at the corner of Benefit and College Streets; it was replaced by the Providence County Court House in 1930.

PROSPECT TERRACE, 2006

In the center of the recent photo a gambrel-roofed house can be seen, but most of the dwellings that were around it in the first photo are now gone. The castle-like structure near the church spire in the first photo, the arsenal for the Providence Marine Corps of Artillery, was built in 1839. It was moved from this location, on Arsenal Lane, to Benefit Street to make way for a train tunnel.

TOCKWOTTEN HOUSE, PROVIDENCE, 1860s

A ghostly figure of a driver, who moved before the photo exposure was finished, stands next to a carriage on the corner of Tockwotten Street, in front of the three-story Doric-columned Tockwotten House. The house was built by James B. Mason (1775–1819), a Federalist who served in the House of Representatives during the 14th Congress, from 1815 to 1817. The house was converted to a hotel when the India Point railroad depot for the New York, Providence & Boston Railroad Company (later the Providence, Warren, & Bristol Railroad) opened nearby, in 1837. In 1850 the City of Providence bought it for use as a reform school. It was demolished in the 1880s, after sitting vacant for several years. The Vartan Gregorian School, once known as the Fox Point School, currently occupies the site.

CITY HOTEL, BROAD STREET (NOW WEYBOSSET STREET), PROVIDENCE, c. 1873, STEREOGRAPH

Delivery wagons and fine carriages wait in front of the City Hotel, one of Providence's finest hotels, which had been converted from a private dwelling. Charles Dyer built a four-story house in the center of what was once a residential area, but by 1832, this section of the city was devoted to business, a transformation that encouraged Dyer to convert his mansion into a hotel. Merchants and politicians stayed there while in town, and supposedly the presidential candidate Stephen Douglas spoke from the second-floor balcony on the left during his campaign against Abraham Lincoln in 1860. In the early 1880s it cost two dollars a night to stay here.

GARNET STREET, PROVIDENCE, LATE 1860s

This photograph of the neighborhood between Weybosset and Friendship streets captured the combination of houses, shops, and mills that are evidence of an area in transition from residential to commercial uses. This area, created on land-filled marshes, is near the site of the present-day Providence Performing Arts Center.

Four men in caps and one in a top hat look straight into the camera near a three-story brick factory building. A notice on the fence reports that the firm Trask & Horton has relocated to 71 Pearl Street. Both the man on the sidewalk and the dog in the road moved as the photographer's slow exposure caught their images. At the end of the wagon-wheel-rutted dirt street, a horse and carriage wait in front of a fish market.

OUR ARCHITECTURAL HERITAGE **PICTURING RHODE ISLAND**

EDDY STREET, PROVIDENCE, c. 1873, STEREOGRAPH

Two identical Second Empire–style houses sit side by side on Eddy Street; each has a separate carriage house in the rear. Both houses were built in 1872, when Eddy Street was residential; now it is now primarily an industrial area. George A. Rickard lived in the one on the left and E. A. Briggs in the one on the right. Two women stand on the front lawn and side entryway porch while one leans out of the open window on the first floor. An enterprising merchant used the plain wooden fencing across the street to advertise his clothing business. Only Rickard's house still stands.

UNIDENTIFIED PROVIDENCE NEIGHBORHOOD, c.1870, STEREOGRAPH BY JAMES W. GOODWIN

In the late nineteenth century, immigrants came to Providence to work in its industries. All over the city, entire neighborhoods of multistory apartment structures were built to accommodate these new residents. A picket fence separates this new cluster of houses from undeveloped land. The smokestack of a factory is in the background. Three people sit on the front steps of the largest dwelling looking at the view.

DEXTER ASYLUM, PROVIDENCE, c. 1875
STEREOGRAPH

In 1824, Ebenezer Knight Dexter donated land and buildings on his farm to the city for the care of the indigent, and by 1828 the building had been erected. Anyone destitute, from abandoned babies to whole families, ended up living at the asylum. By 1957, the building was empty and Brown University purchased it for use as an athletic complex. In this image, the large building is in the background and tilled fields are seen in the foreground.

RESIDENTS OF DEXTER ASYLUM, PROVIDENCE, c. 1900

Residents of the Providence Poor Farm, also known as Dexter Asylum, face the camera at the institution's gates. The wall surrounding the asylum still stands; its original purpose was to protect the working poor from the prying eyes of passers-by.

CORNER OF SPRUCE AND ACORN STREETS, PROVIDENCE, c. 1900

A clothesline full of laundry stretches from the open window of this oddly shaped house in the heart of the Italian section of Federal Hill. All along Acorn and Spruce streets, Italian immigrants settled with fellow-countrymen and opened businesses, creating an Italian-speaking neighborhood within the City of Providence. On this corner an enterprising immigrant bought a lot only six feet wide and forty feet deep, on which he built a multistory house of stucco, stone, and wood. At the rear of the dwelling, a pile of salvaged lumber lies on a platform near a shed and a tall wooden ladder. In the early twentieth century, Atwells Avenue replaced Spruce Street as the center of the Italian community.

NORTH MAIN STREET, PROVIDENCE, c. 1912

In this neighborhood scene in the section of North Main Street known as Constitution Hill, a primarily Jewish neighborhood, a group of barefoot children gather for the excitement of having their picture taken. A tidy girl with a bow in her hair sits in the doorway while the rowdy crowd of boys mills about in front of Kaufman's Boston Bakery. A wagon with a load of other children comes down the hill. On the near side of the street a wagon with a barrel is parked at the curb. On the top of the building, adults watch the activity happening below. Exterior signs advertise Clix and Zira cigarettes, while posters in shop windows announce theatrical performances. This neighborhood is gone, replaced by condominiums.

HENRY BULL HOUSE, NEWPORT, c. 1870, STEREOGRAPH IN "THE BEST SERIES"

A group of children and two men pose in front of the Henry Bull House, an early-seventeenth-century Rhode Island stone dwelling. Bull, a follower of the religious dissident Anne Hutchinson, migrated with her to Portsmouth, Rhode Island, seeking freedom to worship, in 1638. By 1639 he built a house in Newport. The architectural historian Norman Isham thought the original house was one-story with an end chimney. Here it's been enlarged to be a multistory residence with double chimneys. As one of the earliest houses in Newport, it was a landmark until it burned in 1912.

VERNON HOUSE, NEWPORT, c. 1872, STEREOGRAPH BY J. A. WILLIAMS

The photographer Joshua Appleby Williams photographed scenes around Newport and sold them as sets of stereo cards. Here, he captured three boys sitting on the steps of William Vernon's House, at 46 Clarke Street, Newport, built in 1760. A "For Sale" sign on the corner of the building dates the image. At the time of its sale in 1872, the Vernons, a wealthy merchant and banking family, had owned the property for a century. In 1780 and 1781, during the American Revolution, a French general, the Compte de Rochambeau, used the house as his headquarters. In 1782, William Vernon directed that the house be painted using white lead paint and reddish sand so that the wood would look like granite. The Charity Organization Society of Newport bought the building in 1912 to save it from demolition. Today the house is on the National Register of Historic Places.

MATTHEWS MANSION, NEWPORT, c. 1875, STEREOGRAPH BY J. A. WILLIAMS

Nathan C. Matthews of Boston had this "cottage" built in 1871–72 on the corner of Shepard and Bellevue avenues. Designed by the Boston architectural firm of Peabody & Stearns, it is in the Stick style characterized by steeply pitched roofs and decorative elements. Two men dressed in summer white clothes stand near the front steps. It burned in 1881, and Richard Gambrill constructed a new house, Vernon Court, on the site. Today that house is home to the National Museum of American Illustration.

MALBONE PLACE, NEWPORT, 1870s, STEREOGRAPH IN THE SERIES "NEWPORT AND ITS VILLAS," BY E. AND H. T. ANTHONY

The original house on this site was built in about 1741, when the merchant Geoffrey Malbone brought pink sandstone from a quarry in Connecticut to build it. Twenty-two years later it burned to the ground, but much of the granite was still usable. When the New York lawyer Prescott Hall bought the property in 1848 he reused the stone to construct this Gothic Revival–style mansion. When this photo was taken it was owned by Henry Bedlow, a New York resident who became the mayor of Newport. Two women, probably Bedlow's wife and one of his daughters, sit on the lawn under a tree. The man in a tilted hat standing in front of this mansion is possibly Bedlow. The family spent the summer and fall in Newport.

CLIFF VILLAS, c. 1871, STEREOGRAPH BY E. AND H. T. ANTHONY

The smaller villas located near the Cliff Walk Hotel, on Memorial Boulevard, were not as palatial as the mansions on Bellevue Avenue. Built by the Cliff Avenue Cottage Association in 1871, they were summer rentals for seasonal visitors. From this location, residents and guests had easy access to the shore, the Cliff Walk, and other amenities. The Cliff Walk Hotel burned down in 1908, but a few of these dwellings still exist.

BATH ROAD FIRE, NEWPORT, SEPTEMBER 27, 1922

Bath Road once ran from Bellevue Avenue to Easton's Beach, until the construction of Memorial Boulevard. Men dressed in suits and work clothes try to contain a fire in a nearby house and store. They drag a water-filled hose from either a truck or a hydrant located outside this picture frame. In the foreground, a group of African American men carry rescued furniture away from the flames.

HOPELANDS, POTOWOMUT HIGHLANDS, WARWICK, c. 1863

An elderly woman in a day cap stands with two women in fashionable spoon shaped bonnets along with two other women in front of the house that Hope Brown Ives, wife of businessman Thomas P. Ives, called Hopelands. It's likely these women are members of the Ives family living here at the time. A telescope and chair on the front porch may have been used to watch the stars in the evening or the daytime activity on the Potowomut River, which the building overlooks.

The original house consisted of the part on the left, which was occupied by the Greene family in the seventeenth century. "King Richard" Greene, a notorious Tory, died in the house in 1779. Moses and John Brown of Providence bought the house and gave it to their niece, Hope, the daughter of their brother Nicholas and Thomas P. Ives's wife; he enlarged the residence by adding the porch and right-hand side of the dwelling. The Rocky Hill School has used the building since 1948.

ARTHUR FENNER HOUSE, CRANSTON, c. 1875, STEREOGRAPH BY FRANCIS HACKER

Captain Arthur Fenner's dwelling, dating from the seventeenth century, with its large chimney dominates the center of the picture. To the right of the chimney is a later two-story addition that replaced an earlier addition around 1790 and extended the living space. Captain Arthur Fenner (1622-1703) was a follower of Roger Williams; his original residence was burned during King Philip's War of 1675–1676.

Flat board fences surround both the Fenner house and the ancient tree in the front yard. Two men stand in front of the structure. Within fifteen years of this photograph, the house was in ruins and by the end of the nineteenth century it had been torn down.

"STONE CHIMNEY HOUSE," PAWTUCKET, c. 1870 STEREOGRAPH IN THE "PEOPLE'S SERIES OF AMERICAN VIEWS"

In this early spring scene, a young girl pushes a child in a baby stroller in the front yard of this dilapidated seventeenth-century house. The photographer referred to this dwelling as the "Stone Chimney House," but it is unclear to which structure he actually referred. In 1870s Pawtucket, several dwellings constructed by early settlers were still standing. This is possibly the house with a stone chimney that once stood at the corner of Main and Walcott streets.

**JOSEPH JENKS/JENCKES HOUSE, PAWTUCKET,
c. 1875, STEREOGRAPH**

This house belonged to Joseph Jenks, who is credited with being the first settler in Pawtucket, around 1671, and several generations of his descendants lived here. The steeply pitched roof identifies this structure as an early New England saltbox style dwelling.

Two elderly women residents of the house pose for the photographer behind the fence, while a third peers out through an upstairs window. A woman and two boys walking by also stopped for the picture. This house at the corner of North Main near Exchange Street was torn down in 1880, less than ten years after the approximate date of this image.

AMASA SPRAGUE HOUSE, WARWICK, c. 1870

A stable hand holds this stallion still for this photograph of Amasa Sprague's prized possessions—his house and his horses. Sprague built the house in about 1870 in the Valentine Circle area of Warwick, near Post Road. Sprague worked in the family firm of A. & W. Sprague, a well-known textile manufactory that produced calico fabric. Sprague also raised horses and began the Narragansett Trotting Park, which was a turf race track. This house was demolished in about 1930.

HENRY TILLINGHAST SISSON HOUSE, LITTLE COMPTON, 1879–1882

The Sisson family built a house in a new style on the family farm: a three-story Italianate stone building with double porches and a cupola. Colonel Henry Sisson served with General Ambrose Burnside during the Civil War. A statue commemorating Sisson is in the cemetery at Little Compton Commons. On the first-floor veranda four women and a boy pose for the camera. It's likely that one of them is Emily Brownell, Sisson's second wife, and the boy is one of his sons, either David (born in 1875) or Henry (born in 1876). Today the porches are gone, but the house is still standing and is the home of the Stone House Club.

"THE ARNOLD FAMILY, WITH MR. TOURGEE AT THE FENCE IN ALLENTON," c. 1888

Only fifty people lived in the rural village of Allenton around the time this portrait was taken. Allenton was known as the seat of the Baptist church in North Kingstown. The people on the porch are members of the Arnold family, and the man leaning against the fence is a member of the Tourgee family. This two-story farmhouse has a flat-roofed kitchen extension; a barn, fences, and stone walls can also be seen.

BLOCK ISLAND, c. 1870, STEREOGRAPH

This view of Block Island is an extreme contrast to the compactly settled Providence of the 1870s. The Spring House hotel on the right is far away from a cluster of houses on the left. Stone walls mark property lines on the island, the fields are bare of trees. Although only a single hotel is seen here, within a decade over a dozen hotels provided lodging for summer visitors.

ELDERLY WOMAN AT HOME, c.1890

Not everyone lived in perfectly kept houses. This elderly woman smiles for the camera in the screen doorway of her rural house while disrepair surrounds her. From the overgrown weeds in the front yard to the tilted mail box to the missing shingles on the roof, it's obvious that she's on a very limited income in an era before there were benefits for senior citizens. She wears an old-fashioned day cap on her head and her short coat covers her everyday dress and apron. Her gnarled hands reflect a life of hard work.

Nowadays, with a modern transportation infrastructure of highways, high-speed trains, and automobiles, traveling around the nation's smallest state takes no time at all. That wasn't always the case. In the nineteenth century, poor-quality roads and slow vehicles made for long trips.

Waterways such as Rhode Island's rivers and Narragansett Bay often provided a faster way to get from one place to another than overland. Ferry boats and steamers traversed the bay carrying passengers from one side to another or to the shore resorts. Vacationers and others could take the railroad from Boston to Westerly just as they can today, but they could also ride the rails between major Rhode Island towns and down the East Bay.

Individuals journeyed on unpaved roads until the mid-nineteenth century, when cobblestones came into use. Cleaning those new roadways became a necessity, thus creating new jobs. Carriages and horses were the primary conveyance, giving rise to supporting businesses catering to that trade selling buggies and harnesses, just as twentieth-century auto dealers market gas-powered vehicles and the acces-

CHAPTER THREE

GETTING AROUND
On the Water, Traveling the Roads, and Riding the Rails

sories that go with them such as tires. Repair shops fixed four-wheel carriages and, later, automobiles. Traffic backups occurred in nineteenth-century Providence and along mid-twentieth-century Route 1.

Public transportation consisted of stagecoaches until horse-drawn omnibuses and streetcars replaced them. In the late nineteenth and early twentieth centuries, electric trolleys transported folks between home and work or the marketplace.

Throughout the state, bridges were built to span rivers, increasing accessibility and shortening trips. Some, like the Jamestown Bridge, replaced centuries-old ferry routes. In the twentieth century, construction of airports—Theodore Francis Green in Warwick and North Central in Smithfield—enabled individuals to travel even faster from place to place.

The roots of today's mobile generation are preserved in these photographs. Coaches, carriages, rail cars and motor vehicles transported people overland, while marine vessels carried them on water. Despite the obstacles to travel faced by earlier generations, these pictures are evidence that they still managed to get around.

"BOATS ON THE BLACKSTONE RIVER BELOW PAWTUCKET FALLS," c. 1900
PHOTO BY GEORGE W. D. A. DOWNES

Although the original caption reads "Blackstone River," below Pawtucket the river is known as the Seekonk. In the left-hand corner, a shop with a ramp and dock advertises "boats to let." Their skiffs float tied together in the center of picture. Lots of small craft sit at their moorings down the length of the river. A broad tree-lined beach on the bank on the right is in contrast to the mills and roads on the left-hand side of the photo. A dirt road runs past an active factory with smoke pouring from its smokestack. In the background, the Pawtucket Congregational Church and residential neighborhoods are visible.

STEAMER IDA LEWIS, c. 1870, STEREOGRAPH

The early paddle-wheel steamer *Ida Lewis* was named after a nineteenth-century Rhode Island lighthouse keeper, Ida Lewis, who was famous for the rescues she made. One of the three men on board, probably the crew, has his hand on the tiller as the placid waters reflect the boat. On the shore, stacks of logs can be seen in front of a house and barn.

PROVIDENCE HARBOR, c. 1875, STEREOGRAPH IN "THE AMERICAN SCENERY SERIES"

A steam engine's plume blows in the wind over the docks that line Providence Harbor. A ship tied up at the dock is in the process of either being loaded or unloaded. Train cars full of coal sit untended nearby. The area's purpose as a way station for fuel is clear from the sign in the foreground, "Thomas Pearce City Coal Yard." On the other side of the harbor, along Canal Street, is another coal company and the steamer *Richard Borden*.

THE BAY QUEEN, PROVIDENCE, c. 1875
STEREOGRAPH

Every day except Sunday, steamboats left the American Steamboat Company's wharf on Dyer Street for the resorts dotting the shores of Narragansett Bay. On the side of the building behind one of their boats, the *Bay Queen*, is a list of their destinations—Newport, Block Island, Field's Point, and Silver Spring. The paddlewheel of another steamer is visible in the background, as are the houses of the East Side and the spire of the Unitarian Church, formerly the First Congregational Church. The *Bay Queen* was one of the first owned by the company when it started up in 1865. In 1878 the company changed its name to the Continental Steamboat Company.

INTERIOR VIEW OF A STEAMBOAT, 1870s
STEREOGRAPH

Steamer companies spent extravagantly to create a pleasant journey for their customers. Carpets, upholstered furniture, gaslights, drapery and blinds, and architectural details were all part of the experience. Customers on a short ride on the bay or taking an excursion in Long Island Sound enjoyed the luxury.

CREW OF *NEW SHOREHAM*, WASHINGTON SQUARE AT LONG WHARF, c. 1900, EAGLE PHOTO CO.

The Fall River Line was the first steamship company to operate on Narragansett Bay; it was founded in 1828. This steamer in its fleet, the *New Shoreham*, made trips around Narragansett Bay, carrying either passengers or goods. Two lifeboats are positioned atop the vessel's deck. Her crew stands on Newport's Long Wharf in their worn workclothes, though one man in the group, very likely a manager, wears a neatly pressed suit and high-crowned bowler. In 1880, the Fall River Line became the Fall River & Providence Steamboat Company.

SUMMER SCENE, NARRAGANSETT BAY, 1942

By the mid-twentieth century, these weekend sailors chose to travel around the bay in private sailboats and motorboats. Some people ready their boats for a sail around this cove as others watch the action from the pier. Small skiffs on the dock took folks to their moored watercraft or could be used for an afternoon of rowing. This looks like the area near Goddard State Park, in Warwick.

THOMAS W. ARNOLD'S SHOP, 48 DODGE STREET, PROVIDENCE, c. 1874

The sign identifies the business as that of Thomas W. Arnold, carriage painter. Arnold, who we know was forty-three in 1870 from the United States Federal Census, is likely one of the men in this scene. In the front yard of his shop, workmen pose for the photographer surrounded by carriages. On the left, a man in a vest and a half apron stands holding a hammer. Behind him a man in a suit holds a horse steady. In the doorway, a little girl wearing a ruffled dress, jacket, and tilted hat stands next to a man wearing a full overall and high-crowned work cap. Next to him a young man poses with his hands on his hips. Leaning on a carriage wheel is a man holding a mallet resting on his shoulder.

"DEELEY'S," CUMBERLAND, c. 1870, STEREOGRAPH

This photo, labeled "Deeley's," is a bit of a mystery. Photography had many uses in the nineteenth century, just as it does today. The clues in this image lead us to interpret it as a photographic advertisement of goods for sale at this "carriage depository" (see the sign on the roof). The people standing around for the camera are likely a mix of family, employees, and clients. Standing in the foreground, Mr. Deeley poses proudly in front of his wares. Before the automobile and the train, unless one walked, the only way to travel any distance overland involved horses, either riding them or being pulled by them in a buggy or wagon. A full assortment of open buckboard wagons, transom carriages, and coaches were sold at this establishment. The man who climbed up onto the roof has gone to great heights to get into the picture.

KINGSTON, RHODE ISLAND, c. 1900

This town water pump served a dual purpose in the village of Kingston in South Kingston. It gave travelers a chance to stop for a drink and refresh their horses at the trough while the early road signs on top pointed them in the right direction and provided information on distances. The original name of this area was Little Rest.

WATCHEMOKET SQUARE, EAST PROVIDENCE, c. 1900

At this time, the transportation and population center of East Providence was the village of Watchemoket. In the central square of the same name, a wagon driven by an elderly man and a young man crosses the intersection with a full load. A corner market sells a variety of goods as advertised in their windows—hay, grain, flour, and lard. Streetcar tracks run down the middle of the street. On the pole to the right is the bell-shaped emblem indicating that it is a telephone pole. This part of East Providence was once part of Massachusetts; it was annexed to Rhode Island in 1862. Route 95 now runs through the area.

RAILROAD STATION, NEWPORT, c. 1883–88

In front of Newport's train depot, passengers depart the station, walking to their destinations with boxes, purses, and umbrellas in hand. A blanket-covered horse facing the camera is ready to pull an omnibus. At the ticket window a group of young girls crowd together. The station house still exists today, although it is no longer used for trains.

TRAIN AT TIMES SQUARE, PAWTUCKET, c. 1900

Delivery wagons "Stop, Look and Listen" at a central Pawtucket railroad crossing as a train passes by. The Maine Creamery Company canvas-covered wagon with its light-colored horse and painted spokes is in the center of the scene. A station master watches as engine 1506 of the New York, New Haven & Hartford Railroad passes by with its steam engine puffing and its coal car behind the conductor full. Established in 1872, this railroad traveled between New York and Boston. By the early twentieth century it had a transportation monopoly in New England, with diverse holdings in railroads, steamboats, and trolley lines.

DIXON HOUSE, WESTERLY, 1870s

A gentleman reclines in a carriage near Dixon House, a hotel in downtown Westerly. Built of brick, iron, and stone in 1866, it could accommodate three hundred people. Businesses with premises in the hotel included a post office, Pendleton's, E. M. Dunn, Kauders & Company, and A. B. Collins. The hotel's been gone since the 1930s, when it made way for a commercial building, but today Dixon Square derives its name from the original structure.

In the mid-nineteenth century, Rhode Island cities and towns began paving their main thoroughfares with cobblestones. Here, workmen surrounded by piles of cobblestones stop their labors to look over their shoulders at the photographer. To the left of the workmen, a man with a shovel waits near an empty delivery wagon.

PICTURING RHODE ISLAND GETTING ROUND

BROAD STREET (LATER WEYBOSSET STREET) AT ABBOT PARK, PROVIDENCE, c. 1900

In 1891, Broad Street became the first electrified street car route in the city; within three years the last horse-drawn car had been replaced by cabled trolleys. A line of Union Railroad trolley cars loaded with passengers travels up Broad Street, near Abbot Park. Spider webs of electric lines overhead provide power to the trolleys.

Horse-drawn carriages can still be seen parked along the sides of the street, and a number of people on bicycles pedal down the street. Shops along this main thoroughfare advertise their wares on awnings that shade their customers, or on signs painted in prominent places on buildings such as "Monarch Coffee and Tea Set Free." In the background, the Charles S. Bush Company lists its merchandise on a billboard: "chemicals, photographer's supplies, artist's materials, and electrical supplies."

UNION RAILROAD COMPANY STATION, PROVIDENCE, c. 1875, STEREOGRAPH

In 1867, the Rhode Island General Assembly agreed to let the Union Railroad Company construct this depot, and when it was built, most of the railway lines stopped at this waiting room. The building is supported by piles driven into the river on what was known as "the great bridge," near Weybosset Street. A fire destroyed it in 1875, but the company rebuilt it. In 1897 the depot was razed for a bridge-widening project.

In this view, a flatbed freight wagon stops in front of the Union Railroad Depot at 11:30 in the morning, according to the station clock. On the left of the building a man leans on a hitching post while on the right a horse-drawn trolley leaves the area.

MAIN STREET, CHEPACHET, c. 1900

Trolley routes operated in rural communities, bringing residents into the cities, and here can be seen a trolley that had a line from the village of Chepachet in Glocester into Providence. The conductor of the electric street car waits for passengers. On the right a man sits on a bench in front of a Standard Oil Company Service Station that, according to a sign, also sold ice cream. Behind him is a horse and buggy. In the background a car is parked at the curb on the unpaved street.

LOOKING TOWARD MIDDLETOWN, c. 1900

The number 10 trolley, run by the Thomson Houston Electric System, travels down Memorial Boulevard with a full load of passengers. Their destination on this sunny day is Easton's Beach. The pavilion, beach, and walkway can be seen in the background as is the undeveloped landscape of Middletown. Most of the foot traffic is heading down the hill toward the beach, but one woman pushes a shaded stroller up toward town. The beginning of the Cliff Walk is on the right. On a typical summer day in 1913, the trolley from Newport made 194 round trips.

STREET SWEEPER, NORTH MAIN STREET, PROVIDENCE, c. 1911

In the early twentieth century, the Street Cleaning Department, part of the Highway Department of the City of Providence, regulated the repair and cleaning of city streets. In 1911 close to 200 men worked in that capacity. Sweepers wore attire identifying their occupation. In this view, a uniformed African American street sweeper poses with broom in hand near a drain in front of a wagon loaded with beer kegs destined for this bar on North Main Street. In the window are signs advertising a show at the Providence Opera House, listing the types of beer sold (among them Hanley's Peerless Ale), and announcing a fine for spitting on the sidewalk. A little boy walks down the hill to the corner. In the center of the street are tracks for the trolley.

BROADWAY, NEWPORT, c. 1910

Overseers watch men re-lay the train tracks along Broadway in Newport. On the left a man adjusts the track, lifting his head to talk to a supervisor in the background. Next to him a coworker digs with a shovel. Another team further down the road prepares an area for the logs and tracks. On the other side of the construction, the trees are full of coats the hard-working laborers have taken off and hung up.

PICTURING RHODE ISLAND GETTING ROUND

METROPOLITAN RAPID TRANSIT COMPANY BUS, PROVIDENCE, c. 1916

By the second decade of the twentieth century, individuals traveling from Providence to other communities using public transportation could take a trolley or a bus. Buses gradually replaced trolleys beginning in the pre-World War I period. Here, a uniformed female employee of the Metropolitan Rapid Transit Company assists a woman onto the bus in busy Exchange Place. Inside the bus, the driver looks at the photographer. The destination sign across the front of the vehicle states its route: "Pawtuxet via Broad St." A sign on the side requests that customers "pay as they leave." Overhead are advertising posters. In the background a wagon moves quickly by, its wheels a blur.

WASHINGTON STREET, PROVIDENCE, 1951

In this Rhode Island Department of Transportation photo, shirtless workmen labor to remove street car tracks on Washington Street, while two well-dressed women walk by on Empire Street. A policeman stands in the middle of the intersection ready to direct traffic away from the work area.

To the right is the Providence Public Library; alterations to the original 1900 building were ongoing at the time, and a sign mounted on its wall identifies Cimarron Construction as the contractor in charge of the project. In 1953, the library opened its new addition.

MARTIN'S GARAGE, ABORN STREET, PROVIDENCE, c. 1903, PHOTO BY W. A. DEAN

A driver with his foot on the pedal gets ready to pull away from H. G. Martin's shop, which offers automobile storage and repair. In front, mechanics and other owners gather for this picture, while an office employee peers through the glass window near the front door. A proud owner leans on his vehicle in the garage. In addition to fixing these "horseless carriages," Martin advertised in the Providence City Directory that he could store up to one hundred automobiles in his West Exchange Street location. In 1905, the American Locomotive Automobile Company began producing cars in Rhode Island.

PAVING THAMES STREET, NEWPORT, c. 1908

Under the light bulb–studded sign of the Star Theatre and a supersize pipe signaling a tobacco shop, workers lay stone paving on one of Newport's main thoroughfares. Spectators line the sidewalks, where bags of stone are ready for use. After spreading the stone, a steam-powered flattener and a crew of men smooth it out. A steam-driven roller operated by one man then crushes the stone.

SOUTH SIDE OF BRICK MARKET SQUARE IN NEWPORT, 1911

In the early twentieth century, many modes of transportation, both old and new, were being used—this picture shows three of them. Parked at the curb in front of Ringley's Cafe are a bicycle, a horse-drawn delivery cart for Libby's Bakery, and an early automobile. Signs advertize nearby businesses where you can "Rent a Taxi Cab," use the garage, or purchase gasoline. At the bar you can buy Bartholomay's beers and ales.

NARRAGANSETT PARKWAY AT WARWICK DOWNS, c. 1927, PHOTO BY WILFRED STONE

In the late nineteenth century, the landscape architect Frederick Law Olmsted envisioned a national urban park system featuring connecting greenways. Rhode Island's Narragansett Parkway, running through Warwick from the Cranston line to the present-day Route 117, was part of the state's program to create a metropolitan park system modeled after Olmsted's concept in other cities. Beginning in 1912, crews laid out the parkway with a rough gravel surface, which remained until it was paved over in 1927.

In this 1920 shot, cars travel along the Warwick section of the newly paved Narragansett Parkway; two cars are parked on the shoulder, and a trio of walkers strolls on the pathway next to the road.

IMPERIAL THEATRE, BROAD STREET, PAWTUCKET, 1924

On Pawtucket's busy Broad Street, a lone traffic signal in the center of the theater district directs traffic to go slowly and keep right. A boy pulling a wagon walks toward the photographer, while two chatting women follow behind him. The marquee of the Leroy, on the left, which opened on May 1, 1923, proclaims their latest feature, *Girl of the Limberlost*, with a seventeen-star cast, an hour-long movie that premiered in 1924. Across the street the older Imperial Theatre, which opened in 1915, advertises the silent star Charles Ray in *R.S.V.P.*, which premiered in 1921. The Imperial closed in the late 1930s. The Leroy was listed on the National Register of Historic Places, but despite years of failed attempts by various groups to save it, it was demolished in 1997. A Walgreen's now occupies that site.

ROUTE 1 BOTTLENECK, APPONAUG, 1942

By 1942, most families owned cars and the days of minimal traffic were gone, especially on heavily traveled highways such as Route 1, the old Post Road which went from Boston to New York. Already, there was congestion during rush hours, as shown in this photo. At this time, the center of Warwick's business district was the village of Apponaug; here, commuters' cars and a bus stretch far into the distance as they wait their turn to move through the intersection

LASALLE SQUARE, PROVIDENCE, c. 1940

The Firestone Auto Supply & Service Store in LaSalle Square offered customers car repair and a fill-up. Here, cars can be seen driving into the service bays. On the left, a company car is parked next to a pile of tires and a motorcycle. Over the doorway, a banner advertises that the business also sells bicycles. In 1973 this area of the city became home to the public arena called the Civic Center, which has been renamed the Dunkin' Donuts Center.

BRIDGE ACROSS THE WARREN RIVER, 1870s, STEREOGRAPH BY A. G. ELDREDGE

This simple bridge, constructed of wood and iron, connected Warren and Barrington, allowing carriages and people to travel between the towns. A man with a fishing pole hopes for a bite while posing for the photographer. Likewise, a little girl with lunch pail in hand and two young men behind her stop to be in the photograph. On the far side of the bridge, the town side, is a flour and grain repository.

POINT STREET BRIDGE, PROVIDENCE, c. 1872, PHOTO BY LEANDER BAKER

This swing-style drawbridge opened on October 22, 1872, replacing the ferryboats that had carried close to 200,000 people annually from the East Side to Dyer Street. It's been replaced three times since then. At the time, the Point Street Bridge was the fifth span in the city of Providence. Groups of boys and girls gather next to and on the bridge. A hand-painted sign on the bridge's cross bar advised people to "Walk Your Horses Over this Bridge," while a lower notice stated whether the bridge was open for traffic.

BRIDGE OVER THE PAWTUXET RIVER, CRANSTON, c. 1880

From the colonial period to the present day, nine different bridges on this spot have connected the two towns of Warwick and Cranston by spanning the Pawtuxet River. This one was built in 1883, and stands to this day. On the far side are the colonial houses of Warwick and on the near side are the small shops of Cranston. A horse-drawn buggy is about to make its way over the bridge, heading south. In the foreground are the remains of a wooden building, probably an old mill. Two men on the bridge look upriver. A device for controlling the flow of water protrudes from the river near the bank.

Pawtuxet was the site of the burning of the British ship *The Gaspee* just prior to the American Revolution. Each year the village celebrates this event with a parade.

JAMESTOWN BRIDGE, c. 1940

Looming over this extended family group are the concrete supports for the Jamestown Bridge, which spanned the West Passage of Narragansett Bay, connecting Jamestown to North Kingstown. Prior to the building of this span, which opened in 1940, ferryboats carried passengers back and forth several times a day. In the background workers take a break, surrounded by construction equipment and supplies. This bridge itself was demolished on April 18, 2006, and replaced by a newer one.

GETTING AROUND **PICTURING RHODE ISLAND**

T. F. GREEN AIRPORT, WARWICK, c. 1950

Rhode Island's major airport is a very busy place in this photograph, though it might not seem so in comparison to the contemporary scene. Cars drive down Airport Road, parking in the lot on the left. On the right the hangar is in the background and the control tower in the foreground. A single passenger jet is on the runway next to several small engine planes.

The Rhode Island State Airport was laid out in 1929 on 411 acres in the Warwick village of Hillsgrove, and American Airlines began flying from this location in 1932. The airport closed in 1933 to allow for the creation of cement runways, repair of drainage problems, and construction of the buildings seen here. It reopened on May 30, 1936. In 1942, the U.S. Army Air Force took over the airport until 1945, during which time it was known as Hillsgrove Air Base. Civilian service resumed after the war, and in 1945 the airport was renamed yet again, in honor of Theodore Francis Green, a former Rhode Island governor and senator.

NORTH CENTRAL STATE AIRPORT, c. 1953

North Central Airport in Lincoln and Smithfield, which opened in 1951, is one of five airports in Rhode Island. Northeast Airlines began flying to this airport in 1953 and ended service in 1961. A small number of people are seen here waiting on a windy runway for passengers to disembark from a Convair propeller model passenger plane operated by Northeast airlines. A large group of people watch planes take off and land from the open-air observation deck on the second floor of the administration building.

Ask any Rhode Islanders about life in the Ocean State, and they'll tell you stories of going to the shore in the summer. Both Narragansett Bay, which divides the state into two halves, and the Atlantic Ocean provide residents with hundreds of miles of coastline. In the nineteenth century, enterprising individuals in communities with beachfront property capitalized on their natural resource and opened resorts.

Newport, already a tourist spot in the eighteenth century, became a must-see destination in the nineteenth century. Hotels catered to wealthy summer visitors who later became seasonal residents and built mansions. A whole culture and an economy to go with it developed around the practice of spending the summer in the "City by the Sea." Members of the social elite—people with entries in the Social Register—held parties and rode around in coaches in the afternoons. A series of photographs of Easton's Beach over time shows the curve of the water's edge unchanged, but along the shore what was once open landscape became a boardwalk with rides and other resort amenities and entertainments. Enjoying the water thus became a secondary pursuit when one went to the beach.

Elsewhere in the state, wherever there was a beach, people enjoying refreshing ocean breezes

CHAPTER FOUR

ON THE BAY
Recreation and Resorts

and cool water were to be found. Hotels in the town of Narragansett Pier, on the western shore of the bay, provided lodging for affluent out-of-town visitors, as did Jamestown, and the village of Watch Hill, in Westerly. Along the shore of the West Bay, the Rocky Point Amusement Park, on Warwick Point, began offering folks rides and other entertainments in the early nineteenth century. Unlike the other coastal states that had been part of colonial North America, Rhode Island's Royal Charter and Constitution guaranteed public access to the waterline for all.

The highlight of a trip to any point on Narragansett Bay was indulging in a full shore dinner—a clambake prepared by a bake master that was as much spectacle as culinary feast. Native clams and quahog chowder were a standard part of the menu.

Until the hurricane of 1938, Rhode Island held a preeminent spot as a summer playground. The storm changed all that. Wind, rain and flood waters destroyed the resorts and summer communities, and most of them were never rebuilt. These photographs depict a summer lifestyle no longer in existence.

"SILVER POND," NEWPORT, c. 1870, STEREOGRAPH IN "THE AMERICAN SCENERY SERIES," BY J. A. WILLIAMS

Four boys in hats and rolled up pants couldn't resist a summer folic in the shallow water of this pond while their playmate waits on shore. The photographer, Joshua Appleby Williams, named the subject of this photo "Silver Pond," but no body of water by that name appears on nineteenth- or twentieth-century maps of the area. Along the far shore of the pond long wooden ice houses are visible, suggesting that this is actually Lily Pond. It was the only pond with these topographical features where ice was harvested and stored.

VIEW OF NEWPORT HARBOR, c. 1870, STEREOGRAPH BY MARINE VIEWS

This young man crouches down and stares into the camera dressed in a loose-fitting coat, silk tie, and flat-topped hat. On the right, latticed open gates flank the road leading to this spot, which may indicate that it was a private estate. Across the water is downtown Newport.

DIGGING CLAMS AT MISQUAMICUT, c. 1925

Misquamicut is an ocean-front community on Block Island Sound, in the town of Westerly, near the Connecticut state line. The lack of roads in this area discouraged development; the first summer house wasn't built until 1894 and by 1903 only an additional twenty-eight houses had been built. The resort grew rapidly in the twentieth century, only to be destroyed when the hurricane of 1938 washed away four hundred beach-front houses.

    Here, rakes in hand, two boys in shirts and ties and two girls in dresses dig up the sand at low tide, looking for clams. The seven miles of beach at Misquamicut gave these industrious children plenty of opportunity to fill their pail in time for supper.

ON THE BAY **PICTURING RHODE ISLAND**

OCEAN HOUSE, NEWPORT, c. 1870, STEREOGRAPH BY JOHN P. SOULE

Ocean House, seen across the wide expanse of Bellevue Avenue, was a first-class hotel and a much-copied symbol of high-class tourism in the nineteenth century. This 1846 Gothic-inspired structure was not the first Ocean House; the original Ocean House burned down in 1845, only a year after being built. The new building, erected in one year, was bigger and better than its predecessor. The new five-story hotel featured 250 feet of frontage along Bellevue Avenue and accommodations for over four hundred guests.

OCEAN HOUSE FROM THE SIDE, c. 1870, STEREOGRAPH BY J. A. WILLIAMS

An avenue of trees cast shadows over the carriage paths on the Bellevue Avenue side of Ocean House, while porches with decorative elements and shaded oversize windows, open to the ocean breezes, shielded guests from the sun. Guests enjoyed generously laid out bedrooms, a frescoed dining room, and modern conveniences such as bathrooms and electric bells. Fire destroyed the structure in 1898; a shopping plaza occupies the spot today.

U.S. HOTEL, 184 THAMES STREET, NEWPORT, STEREOGRAPH

Men in work clothes lean against the corner of the building on the right, while a well-dressed coachman in a top hat waits for passengers in his open carriage. Other men in the doorway peer out at the photographer. Shuttered windows allowed patrons to block out the light or let in the sea air. Across the street a liquor dealer sells champagnes and claret.

STROLLING ON EASTON'S BEACH, NEWPORT, 1860s, BY J. A. WILLIAMS

Named for Nicholas Easton, one of the original settlers in Newport, even in the eighteenth century Easton's Beach was a favorite spot for visitors; two prominent visitors were the Anglican bishop, George Berkeley, and the merchant Francis Malbone. In this busy scene, two women stroll along the walkway, using parasols to protect their skin from the sun. A group of children occupy the path in front of them. Near the house in the background, a coach discharges passengers. On the beach itself small carriages carry people along the shoreline. Other individuals wade into the water in voluminous bathing costumes. Sparsely populated Middletown is visible beyond the beach.

CARRIAGES ON EASTON'S BEACH, NEWPORT, c. 1880, PHOTO BY KILBURN BROS.

A man in his shaded horse-drawn buggy waits for passengers, while a family group surrounds a cart drawn by a donkey. Visitors could drive their buggies down the length of the beach or hire carriages to transport them at the shore. In the background, scores of people can be seen enjoying the refreshing ocean water.

BATH HOUSE AT EASTON'S BEACH

Easton's Beach was a public beach that was used by visitors from all economic classes. This bath house, built in 1886, contained drawing rooms, a café, two bandstands, and five hundred bathing rooms that offered users a choice of hot, cold, or seawater showers. In this picture, a fashionably dressed little boy and girl have stopped to gaze at the photographer. On the porch, men, women, and children enjoy the beach shaded from the sun. A few stroll across the sand or down the planked walkway to the water's edge.

NEWPORT BEACH, c. 1917

By 1917, Easton's Beach had became known as Newport Beach; the quaint Gothic Revival bath house was gone, replaced by this expansive twin-towered complex. Behind the right urn-topped tower is the indoor carousel, which even today remains an attraction for visitors to this beach.

"ROMAN GARDEN", NEWPORT BEACH, 1930s

An outdoor pool complex called the Roman Garden was built adjacent to the meadows of Aquidneck Island in Narragansett Bay. In this photo from the thirties, men, boys, and young women stand around the perimeter of the Roman Garden's pool watching a water race. Its high diving platform attracted adventuresome athletes like the people lying down or leaning over the edge to better see swimming events in the pool. Beyond the pool, the parking lot is packed on this summer's day.

OLD MILL ROLLER COASTER, NEWPORT, 1930s

The Old Mill Roller Coaster's gut-dropping descents and the thrills experienced on its wooden rails helped contribute to Newport Beach's reputation as "the Quality Resort of the East." A tired boy in a bathing suit frowns into the camera, the only person dressed for the beach. All the action in this scene is taking place on the boardwalk crowded with fully dressed individuals. The roller coaster wasn't the only entertainment; the well-known pilots Jack McGee and Ruth Law often made flights over the beach to amuse swimmers. The 1938 hurricane destroyed the most of the amusements at Easton's Beach including the pool and the roller coaster.

EASTON'S BEACH, 1930s

In this photo from the 1930s, taken near the location of nineteenth-century views seen earlier, cars are parked bumper to bumper on Memorial Boulevard, near Easton's Beach. Much has changed in seventy years. A paved sidewalk and railing allow for leisurely walks at the shore, and a couple is seen walking arm in arm. In the foreground two men in twentieth-century bathing costumes stand on the beach, and other bathers are visible farther down the beach and in the water. The entertainment complex and roller coaster, which newspapers of the day raved about, are barely visible on the far left. In the background is St. George's School in Middletown.

EASTON'S BEACH, 1950s

After the hurricane of 1938, which destroyed the beach houses, the roller coaster, and the boardwalk, visitors turned to the simpler pleasures of sunning themselves on the beach or sitting under umbrellas. Rhode Islanders rebuilt the pavilion at Newport Beach using sturdier building materials and constructed a concrete sea wall to protect the area from storms. Today, Rhode Island natives refer to this section of shoreline as Easton's Beach, Newport Beach, or First Beach, all names alluding to its historic reputation.

CLAMBAKE AT EASTON'S BEACH, 1909

Hot steam is blown by the wind into the face of the bake master, the chief cook in charge of tending a traditional Rhode Island clambake, as he throws a bucket of water on the hot layers of food embedded in seaweed. Clambakes took place outside; the layers of seafood (clams, lobster, and fish), sweet corn, and sausages are steamed using hot rocks and seaweed. On the left, a helper carries a pan of more food to place on the pile. Another assistant doffs his hat while another man in an apron keeps an eye on the clams and tin plates of food cooking on the top. Empty buckets nearby are ready to be filled with additional water. In 1882, the typical cost of one of these shore dinners, offered by beach-front resorts around Narragansett Bay, was fifty cents per person..

PURGATORY CHASM, PROBABLY MID-1860s, STEREOGRAPH IN "THE AMERICAN SCENERY SERIES," BY MARINE VIEWS

The small size of the figure peering down into the 160-foot drop of Purgatory Chasm, in Middletown, gives a sense of the scale and the danger as waves wash into the crack in the rocks near Easton's Point, eroding the sides. The Rhode Island historian Welcome Arnold Greene wrote in 1886 that "to stand on the high rocks and gaze into the chasm upon the turmoiling waters below, is a severe test of steadiness and nerve." The sparse vegetation seen here has expanded so that brush now covers the crevice; a wooden bridge allows visitors to walk over the chasm.

MRS. CADWALADER'S ARCH, NEWPORT, c. 1870, BY J. A. WILLIAMS

General George Cadwalader (1806–1879) and his wife, Frances, once owned the property around Rough Point later owned by Doris Duke. General Cadwalader was a nineteenth-century military figure whose actions during the Mexican War and the Civil War had brought him renown. This stone arch, on Cliff Walk, was built by Mrs. Cadwalader, and may be one of two still standing on the Cliff Walk. Its boulder- and grass-covered surface attracted visitors looking to climb to the top for a view of the bay or pass through it on a stroll along the shore. In this photo, a man walks beneath this stone arch along the Cliff Walk, while a woman sits atop it.

GROUP ON THE CLIFF WALK, NEWPORT, c. 1900

Cliff Walk is a three-and-a-half-mile path along the water's edge that leads past the mansions built by New York's wealthy who summered in Newport. Originally it was an unpaved track used by fishermen. The wealthy abutters tried several times in the last 150 years to restrict access by the public, but enshrined in the state's constitution is the right to walk along the shore. In this view, four couples enjoy an afternoon's outing along the walking trail.

COACHING PARTY IN FRONT OF THE CASINO ON BELLEVUE AVENUE, NEWPORT, c. 1888, PHOTO BY E. M. BIDWELL

Newport's Casino, designed by McKim, Mead and White, was completed in 1881. It was a center of the social life in town with its grass and court surface tennis courts and gaming rooms. In this view, a coaching party pauses in front of the Casino, the horses being held by a groomsman wearing a top hat, gloves, and tails. Another in similar dress and wearing a corsage sits on top of the coach holding the reins; next to him sits a well-dressed woman. Behind her several men in round-crowned hats and straw boaters converse with the women next to them. It was part of a regular set of events prescribed by Mrs. William Backhouse Astor, a leading Newport hostess. Afternoon coaching processions around town followed by evening balls and parties exhibited the economic status and social position of Newport's summer residents.

NEWPORT HORSE SHOW, c. 1900, PHOTO BY ALVIAN AND CO.

A man sitting in a lightweight carriage looks to his right, while a woman in a polished carriage with a running board, folded top, and headlight talks to a man to her left. Both horses look poised to race. Under the canopy the crowd waits for the event to begin. In front, a man in top hat, tails, and high boots stands ready to give the signal to start.

OAKLAND BEACH, c. 1870, STEREOGRAPH BY G. N. LOMBARD

Oakland Beach was a famous resort community on the western shore of Narragansett Bay in what is now Warwick. In this view, men in Native American costumes paddle their canoes across a narrow part of Oakland Beach as they participate in some kind of historical reenactment, while other men watch from a bench on the shore. Tents in the background supply housing for these campers. Decades later, Oakland Beach's 116 acres featured a hotel and a water toboggan ride. By 1937 little remained of the resort. Summer dwellings became permanent residences, and new developments turned the area into a neighborhood of small cottages and stores.

APPONAUG, c. 1871, STEREOGRAPH BY J. H. AYLESWORTH

Two women wearing bathing costumes consisting of long dresses with close-fitting pants along with bare-chested men and boys cool off in the waters of Narragansett Bay. With the exception of one woman on the left, everyone stops to look at the photographer. One man proudly poses in his striped bathing outfit. Fully attired men women and children cluster on the shore. Visible in the background is one of the two churches once located in Apponaug, a village in the town of Warwick. At one time the town also had a single hotel and was home to the Oriental Print Works, which made woolen yarn. In the 1880s only seven hundred people lived here, but residents optimistic about their future thought that "Apponaug will yet be bigger than London." Today, the village is the administrative center of the town of Warwick.

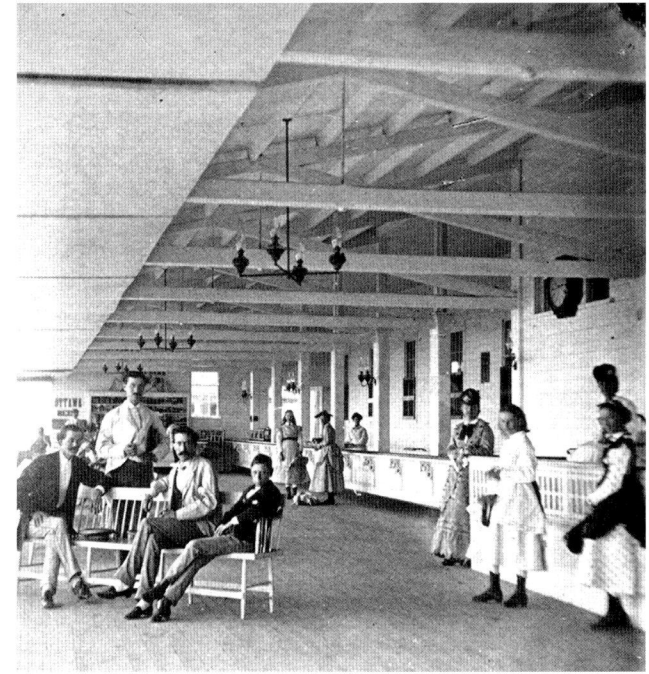

THE SHED, ROCKY POINT, 1870s, PHOTO BY J. A. WILLIAMS

The Rocky Point Shore Dinner Hall accommodated a thousand people for its famous clam cakes and chowder. Two of the park's African American employees, one a waiter identified by his jacket, stand on the steps of a building near a ticket pavilion known as The Shed, where tickets for the shore dinner—it cost fifty cents—were sold. A man in a silk top hat and a man in a straw hat, and two men dressed casually without jackets wait in line to buy their tickets. Another man leans against the sign.

THE "PORCH" AT ROCKY POINT, c. 1876, STEREOGRAPH

A photographer caught this small group gathered for shade, refreshments, and food on the "Porch" at the Park. Behind the counter, a woman is ready to take orders while visitors lean against railings or rest on benches. Root beer first became available about 1876, and one can see at the far end a soda fountain that sells Ottawa beer, a type of root beer typically made with sugar, snake-root, and aromatics. It was kept on tap in the summer. Gaslight lanterns suspended from the ceiling provided illumination in the evening.

OBSERVATORY AT ROCKY POINT, 1870s, STEREOGRAPH

Adventurous guests could climb the winding stairways to the top of the ten-story high observatory to peer out its many windows. At 250 feet above sea level, guests gazed out toward the west side of Narragansett Bay from its Warwick location and on a clear day could see sights as far away as Newport.

GUEST HOUSES AT ROCKY POINT, 1870s, STEREOGRAPH BY J. H. AYLESWORTH

Men face the camera from the grounds surrounding a lodging house at Rocky Point. A three-tiered fountain decorates a fenced-in garden. Between the buildings stands a smaller structure with "shop" written above the door. In the foreground, a worker in high boots walks along the rocks carrying a bucket in each hand.

DOCK AT ROCKY POINT, 1870s

Guests arrived at Rocky Point by private boat, train, and steamboat (later also by trolley car). Long docks at Rocky Point accommodated the steamboats that made hourly stops at the park. The paddle-wheel steamer *Canonicus*, which could carry eleven hundred people, waits for passengers traveling to locations around the Bay.

BOATING AT ROCKY POINT, 1870s, STEREOGRAPH BY J. H. AYLESWORTH

Visitors at Rocky Point had their choice of activities in the Park or on the water. Boat rentals let guests go for a sail on the bay on a sunny, breezy afternoon. In what may have been a shot staged for the photographer, ten people on board a catboat face the camera. The man seated in the stern manages the sail's sheet with one hand and has his other hand on the tiller.

WATER VIEW OF ROCKY POINT, c. 1900

Rocky Point was a popular and old Rhode Island resort, located in Warwick, that in 1918 was known as "New England's Most Beautiful Amusement Park." In the early eighteenth century a Captain William Winslow bought all the land in the area and began building a resort with rides and a dining hall. The American Steamboat Company bought the park in 1869 and developed it into a major tourist attraction. In 1877, Rutherford B. Hayes made the first telephone call ever placed by an American president, from Rocky Point to Professor Alexander Graham Bell at the City Hotel in Providence. In the early 1880s, the resort had its own summer newspaper to keep guests informed of the program. A fire in 1883 destroyed many of the buildings, including the hotel, but all were rebuilt. Then, the hurricane of 1938 destroyed the roller coaster, most of the rides, and the dining hall. It took ten years to completely rebuild the resort. But by the nineties, increased operating costs and declining numbers of visitors led to the eventual closure of the park in 1995.

This undated water view of Rocky Point shows the boat launch, carousel, roller coaster, observatory, and guest houses. By the time this picture was taken, in the early 1900s, Rocky Point was an entertainment hub with live shows, a wide range of rides such as a steam-powered Ferris wheel seen here near the bicycle rental shed, and lodgings such as the building to the right on the hill.

88 NARRAGANSETT CASINO, NARRAGANSETT PIER, c. 1890, BY WILLIAM MILLS

The casino at Narragansett Pier was designed by the notable late-nineteenth-century architectural firm of McKim, Mead & White, and Frederick Law Olmsted landscaped the grounds. It took three years, 1883-1886, to finish this resort, where guests could play billiards or tennis, bowl, or enjoy the shore. Patrons dined at its restaurants, shopped at the stores, or relaxed by watching theatrical or musical performances. All this came to an end with a fire on September 12, 1900, which began at the nearby Rockingham Hotel. It destroyed part of Narragansett Pier, including the casino. McKim, Mead & White designed a replacement, which opened on July 8, 1905. Today all that remains of the Narragansett Casino are the towers.

At one thirty-five on a summer's afternoon, diners sit under the casino's striped umbrellas. Surreys wait on a nearby street and in the shade of the stone arch for passengers. An opening in the stone wall near the beach provides access to the rocky shore.

**CROQUET AT A HOTEL IN NARRAGANSETT PIER,
1869-1875, STEREOGRAPH**

The seaside resort of Narragansett Pier acquired its name from a long pier that once extended into the water and served as a landing place for steamboats and other vessels. Eventually surf destroyed the pier, but the area retains the name. In the late nineteenth century Narragansett Pier was known as "a city of hotels"; like Newport, it catered to a wealthy clientele. The Narragansett Pier Railroad operated a short eight-and-half-mile line that ran along the shoreline and made stops at Kingston, Peace Dale, Wakefield, and Narragansett Pier. It ceased operations in the 1950s.

In front of this Narragansett Pier hotel, guests engage in a variety of activities. To the left, a boy poses next to a group of girls holding dolls. Adults and one child take a break from their game of croquet, mallets in hand. Croquet first became popular in the United States in the 1860s as a game that men and women could play together. An elderly woman and a couple of boys watch the match close to the action, while other guests peer from the shade of the veranda. The man sitting on the grass in the foreground feeds a bird in a cage.

90 **OCEAN HOUSE, WATCH HILL, c. 1870,
STEREOGRAPH BY FRANCIS HACKER**

In this 1870s stereo view of one of Watch Hill's premier hotels, guests and staff crowd the porch and balcony for the photographer. The first hotel in Watch Hill was built in the 1840s, but forty years later there were seven hotels, with names such as the Atlantic House, Larkin House, and the one depicted here—Ocean House, named after the famed Newport hotel. It was built in 1868 and was demolished in 2005.

POINT JUDITH LIGHTHOUSE, NARRAGANSETT, c. 1874, STEREOGRAPH

Several young people—three women, a man and two children—pose on the lawn in front of the Point Judith Lighthouse erected in 1816. Behind the lighthouse itself is the house that was built in 1857 as a residence for the lighthouse keeper and his family. To the left is the assistant keeper's house, built in 1874. A stack of logs and other wood refuse (a wheel is visible) provide fuel for the facility. On the far left, the chimney of the building housing the Daboll fog signal, powered by a hot-air engine, stands ready to blow in inclement weather. Both houses have been replaced by twentieth-century structures that were built by the Coast Guard. The lighthouse still exists today, but its upper story has been painted brown.

VIEW FROM WATCH HILL, 1870s, STEREOGRAPH

Two docks extend from a Watch Hill beach. The crew of a paddle-wheel steamboat with flags waving in a strong Narragansett Bay breeze stand on one pier looking for passengers. Three small gaff-rigged sailboats with occupants get ready to head out into the bay for an afternoon outing.

"WHERE THE BREAKERS ROLL IN ON THE SAND," WATCH HILL, WESTERLY, c. 1938

This title of this photo says it all. Watch Hill was famous for its beaches, which swept seven miles to the west to Napatree Point. Summer residents built their summer cottages, like the ones shown here, on the beach amid the dune grass. On this cloudy summer day two people sit under an umbrella on their front yard of beach sand. Watch Hill sustained tremendous damage from the 1938 hurricane. On Napatree Point, thirty-nine cottages, their owners' cars, and the road all disappeared, swept out to sea or into Watch Hill Harbor.

ON THE BEACH, WATCH HILL, c. 1930

On a sunny summer's day, groups of bathers and sun worshipers cluster under umbrellas in all modes of beach attire. The young women in tank suits in the foreground converse while their male companion, in a masculine version of the same suit, sits quietly nearby. Fully dressed older women sit in on the sand, their cloche hats shielding their faces from the sun. Further down the beach, a man talks with a woman in a dress in front of children playing in the sand with pails and shovels. Today, this area is a conservation area.

LOBSTERMEN AT FORT DUMPLINGS, c. 1870, PHOTO BY J. A. WILLIAMS

The ruins of Fort Dumplings were on an island in Newport Harbor. Colonists first used the granite cliffs of Conanicut Island, known as Dumpling Rock, for an earthen fortification for defense of Newport Harbor and the East Passage of Narragansett Bay. During the American Revolution, the British captured the fort during their occupation of Newport and called it Fort Dumpling Rock. After that war, Americans built a stone tower on the site, mounted with eight guns, but later abandoned it in favor of Fort Adams in Newport. In 1898 the United States destroyed the tower ruins and created Fort Wetherill on the site.

Lobstermen near their empty pots look across a cove at the ruins. The man on the right holds a horseshoe crab upside down by its tail.

MT. PLEASANT GROUP, SUNDAY SCHOOL EXCURSION, JAMESTOWN, c. 1905

Rhode Islanders of all economic classes visited Jamestown. Individuals, families, and organizations like this Sunday School group of women and girls from the Providence neighborhood of Mt. Pleasant took day trips to walk the beach and picnic. A little girl behind this group walks the shore looking for shells.

FERRY LANDING, JAMESTOWN, c. 1890

In 1695, ferry service was established to bring people from Saunderstown in North Kingstown and from Newport to Jamestown. Farming was the primary economic activity on the island until the latter half of the nineteenth century, when wealthy patrons from the Philadelphia area started building summer residences there. Two hundred years later the town still centered on the landing, but a sign on the woman's left advertising farms for sale, furnished cottages for rent, and building sites is evidence of the demographic change on the island in the late nineteenth century. Those not able to have their own summer home on the island stayed at several large hotels and guest houses that catered to a wealthy clientele. In the background is the Bay View Inn.

Today, thousands of people from all over the world come to Providence to see the award-winning public sculpture called Waterfire, a bonfire display with musical accompaniment. In the nineteenth century, the city had a reputation for Fourth of July celebrations that began with cannons at dawn and balloon ascensions.

Everyday life in Rhode Island cities and towns in the past wasn't without fun and excitement. Children amused themselves by scampering around neighborhoods and climbing natural formations. In warm weather, people went outdoors to East Providence's resorts such as Silver Spring and amusement parks such as Crescent Park and Vanity Fair. Quieter times could be found at Providence's Roger Williams Park, which provided visitors plenty of ways to spend an afternoon by either walking its pathways or paddling around a number of small lakes. Also in the city, Park Garden held spectacular theatrical performances in the city's first electric light park.

Indoor entertainment options abounded. The Pawtucket Theatre, the Providence Opera House, Newport's Bijou, and other theaters offered live performances until they were converted to movie houses. Huge venues such as Providence's Infantry

CHAPTER FIVE

OUT ON THE TOWN
City Amusements

Hall seated thousands for concerts, speeches, and sporting events.

Parades were organized and triumphal arches were erected to commemorate patriotic, historic, and nostalgic occasions such as the Fourth of July, the Cotton Centennial, and Old Home Week. Displays of red, white, and blue bunting accompanied these events. The state's largest public demonstration, the Preparedness Day Parade, which wound through downtown Providence and featured a living flag of colorfully dressed schoolchildren, took place prior to World War I. World War I also brought the sale of Liberty bonds in support of the war, from "Liberty Bell"–shaped stations constructed of fabric and set up in public places. Arches spanned roads to celebrate Samuel Slater's cotton manufacturing industry, the four hundredth anniversary of Columbus's voyage to America, and the two hundred fiftieth anniversary of the founding of Pawtucket.

Photographs of the past show crowds of people enjoying themselves by participating in a variety of events. City and town life wasn't dull. Opportunities to mingle with friends, family, and neighbors were around every urban corner.

BALLOON ASCENSION, PROVIDENCE, c. 1866, STEREOGRAPH BY FRANCIS HACKER

Crowds gather around a hot-air balloon named the *Monarch* in this Providence scene from 1866. Men grip the netting at the bottom of the balloon that holds it down to earth. This event took place on an empty triangular lot where the Providence City Hall now stands. To the left is the Union Passenger Depot with ranks of wagons and horse-drawn trolley cars parked in front. In the background the spire of the First Baptist Church is visible.

The city became famous in the nineteenth century for featuring balloon ascensions as part of its Fourth of July celebrations. In the first such ascension, in 1800, the passengers in the basket were a dog and a cat. A local celebrity, Professor James K. Allen, and his son experimented with balloons in Providence before and after the Civil War. During the War the Allens flew surveillance balloons for the Union Army, under the command of General Ambrose Burnside.

ABBOTT PARK, PROVIDENCE, c. 1875, STEREOGRAPH BY LEANDER BAKER

This small park is still in existence in downtown Providence, now surrounded by tall office buildings, but this is just what the donor of the park intended. Daniel Abbott, a Providence merchant and landowner, gave land to the Congregational Church to build a place of worship on what was then Broad Street. He then presented an additional 7,800 square feet of open land to the city, stipulating in his gift that it was "for public use, passing and repassing, training and the like, always to be free from any buildings forever." Known over the years by various names (the Old Common, Abbott Parade, and Abbott Park), this little park remains a monument to one man's vision. This photograph was taken to commemorate the iron fountain presented to the city of Providence in 1875 by a group of businessmen.

STATUE OF ROGER WILLIAMS IN ROGER WILLIAMS PARK, c. 1877 STEREOGRAPH BY LEANDER BAKER

Dressed for an afternoon's outing in dark-colored dresses, hats, and parasols, three women pose in front of the newly dedicated—in 1877—statue of Roger Williams in the park of the same name. The Williams family owned the 103 acres until 1871, when a descendant of Williams's, Betsey Williams, donated it to the city with the stipulation that the city build a memorial to her ancestor. The sculptor Franklin Simmons designed the twenty-seven-and-a-half-foot-tall granite and bronze monument, which cost $18,500, an astounding sum at the time.

WHAT CHEER COTTAGE, ROGER WILLIAMS PARK, PROVIDENCE, c. 1878, STEREOGRAPH BY LEANDER BAKER

Patrons waiting for the trolley home after a day at the Park could rest and enjoy refreshments in the What Cheer Cottage (its name derived from the greeting of the Narragansett Indians to Roger Williams, "What Cheer, Netop") built by the Union Horse Railroad Company and completed around 1878, about the time this photo was taken. It shows a first-floor porch and second-floor balcony, where women are seen holding parasols to shield themselves from the sun. While their mothers watch from the shade, children folic on a summer's afternoon, staring at photographer Leander Baker while he takes this picture.

OUT ON THE TOWN   **PICTURING RHODE ISLAND**

BOATING IN ROGER WILLIAMS PARK, LATE 1870s

Visitors to the Roger Williams Park could visit the zoo, stroll the gardens, or rent a boat to row around Crystal Lake. In the foreground of this picture a man takes a drink from the water bucket, which was drawn up from the well by means of a cantilevered wooden pole and rope. In the background watercraft line the shore of one of the park's ponds. A wooden footbridge and wide paths are perfect invitations for an afternoon walk around the water's edge.

BOATING, ROGER WILLIAMS PARK, c. 1900

The park offered numerous opportunities for relaxation, and over a quarter of its acreage consists of lakes and lagoons. The park's many bodies of water also offered opportunities for private and romantic moments in an earlier age. This couple may have rented a boat with just such an idea in mind. The young woman reclines in the boat and shades herself with her parasol, as her companion, in a straw hat and suit, rows them around the lake.

HMS PINAFORE PERFORMED AT PARK GARDEN, PROVIDENCE, 1879, STEREOGRAPH BY A. E. ALDEN

The Park Garden was a thirteen-acre urban amusement park on Broad Street owned by David Wallis Reeves, of the nationally famous American Brass Band, and John R. Shirley, who opened it on June 24, 1878. Visitors explored the lakes, paths, and gardens of this metropolitan playground during summer. Guests could ride in the Venetian-style gondolas, stop for a cool treat at the ice cream pagoda, or participate in an amusement called Robinson Crusoe's Hut. They could also enjoy theatrical extravaganzas performed in the open air. Here, the costumed cast of Gilbert and Sullivan's comic operetta, *The HMS Pinafore* or *The Lass That Loved a Sailor*, face the camera on board the 110-foot ship built for the production. A hundred chorus members and a twenty-eight-piece orchestra provided the music for this show, which ran for thirteen weeks during the summer of 1879. Four cast members stand on a spar in the ship's rigging.

PARK GARDEN BOAT HOUSE, c. 1879, STEREOGRAPH BY A. E. ALDEN

Four oarsmen await customers near the park's boathouse. The park closed in 1883.

CRESCENT PARK, EAST PROVIDENCE, c. 1890

On a hot summer day, you could "shoot the chutes" at Crescent Park, as these young men were waiting their turn to do. In 1886, George Boyden built Crescent Park adjacent to the Bullock's Point Hotel in Riverside to provide guests access to the area's accommodations and fun. Crescent Park featured the "Riverboat Ride" (an inside thrill ride), and a carousel with horses carved by Charles I. D. Loof; Loof bought the park in 1920. Boyden's Vanity Fair lasted only a few years, but Crescent Park remained in business under a series of owners until the 1970s. The carousel, maintained by the Crescent Park Carousel Commission, is still open.

SILVER SPRING HOUSE, EAST PROVIDENCE, c. 1880, STEREOGRAPH

Silver Spring, Golden Spring, Riverside, Cedar Grove, Bullock's Point, and Camp White. Visitors to these destinations came to enjoy breezes off the water and the shore dinners. The two wide verandas of this house encouraged guests like the group gathered on the second-floor in this photo to rest and relax, and one of the gentlemen below them to perch on the railing over the water.

VANITY FAIR, EAST PROVIDENCE, c. 1907

Under a striped canopy, Fay's American Band plays music to a few people at Vanity Fair amusement park, another urban playground. Modeled after Wonderland at Revere Beach, north of Boston, it cost $750,000 dollars when it opened on Memorial Day, 1907, on forty acres in East Providence. Entertainments along the boardwalk included "Tours of the World" for ten cents and "Over the Rockies." In this view, hungry patrons wait under an awning for a shore dinner or buy a five-cent bottle of Moxie from Bernardini's stand.

In its advertising the park's management referred to Vanity Fair as the "all electric park"; admission cost ten cents. Attractions included water chutes as well as a public ballroom and a Japanese tea room. An unusually sensational display called "Fighting the Flames" took place every day. It involved the actual burning of a house, the rescue of its occupants—staff positioned at the windows of the structure jumped into nets—and the extinguishing of the flames. A Wild West show featured fifteen American Indians, twenty-five cowboys, and fifty horses. Visitors could ride in chutes between the park's towers to view Narragansett Bay, or visit the "Hunan Laundry" (a fun house) or the "Dippy Daffy House." Rhode Islanders didn't have any trouble getting to Vanity Fair. Trolley cars labeled "Vanity Fair" carried people from Fox Point in Providence and steamers took people up the bay. The cost of maintaining the exhibits and competition in the area led to the closure of the park two years after it opened. A fire in 1912 destroyed it. Today there is an oil terminal on this site.

GLACIER ROCK, SKY HIGH HILL, ATWELLS AVENUE, PROVIDENCE, c. 1915.

Neighborhood landmarks such as this enormous rock provided children of all ages a place to play, climb, or pose for a formal picture. Wearing their Sunday best, these children range in age from the baby in the stroller on the left to the older boys standing as far from the camera as possible. Older girls cared for the younger children; here one older girl is seen holding the hands of a younger child, perhaps to keep her still for this group portrait, from the World War I decade.

OPERA HOUSE, PROVIDENCE, c. 1871, STEREOGRAPH

A man in a silk top hat looks across Dorrance Street at the Providence Opera House. Directly opposite, two men engage in conversation near a grocery and provision shop. Near the front entrance you can see piles of cobblestones and the blurs of workmen busy paving the street. The construction of this landmark only took ninety days. Dedicated on November 4, 1871, the theater remained open for sixty years, though did not remain an opera house. The space could accommodate up to 1,500 people for operas and, later, vaudeville shows and movies. On August 16, 1915, a full house saw D. W. Griffith's movie, *The Birth of a Nation*.

INFANTRY HALL, PROVIDENCE, c. 1926

In 1879, the Providence Light Infantry Association spent $60,000 to build Infantry Hall, on South Main Street. This enormous building housed stores on the first floor. In the center, one of its tenants, a grocer, is seen securing the awning. On the second and third floors were rooms for veteran groups and businesses as well as a dining room. In the rear of the building was an auditorium with a seating capacity of two thousand; it was used for diverse entertainments and events such as presidential speeches (McKinley, Teddy Roosevelt, and Taft all spoke here), as well as musical concerts and prize fights. Association members used the fourth floor for their activities; it also housed an armory, an officers' room, a club room, a library and a reading room. Infantry Hall closed in 1926 and remained vacant until a fire destroyed it in 1942.

106 NEW PAWTUCKET THEATRE, PAWTUCKET, 1904-1908

As men and boys exit the theater, playbills affixed to the façade of the turreted New Pawtucket Theatre building, at 133 High Street, on the corner of Exchange Street, announce the current show, *The Great Romantic Melodrama Monte Cristo*, and future entertainments, including *The King of Forgers*. The New Pawtucket Theater opened in 1904 and remained in business until 1908, when it became a Fay's theater and then closed.

THE BIJOU THEATRE, NEWPORT, c. 1900

In the early twentieth century, nearly every city had a vaudeville and movie house, and Newport had the Bijou, located at 192 Thames Street. It was just one of the theaters offering indoor diversions to tourists and residents of the area. The marquee advertised a 10 cent admission price. A sign on the second floor indicates that the Army and Navy Y.M.CA occupied space above the theater.

PARADE IN WARREN, c. 1875, STEREOGRAPH BY A. G. ELDREDGE

A. G. Eldredge took this picture of a band marching in a parade near his studio in Warren; his business sign is visible on the right side of the photo. Residents on the sidewalk near the photographer watch him take the image, while those farther down keep their eyes on the action in the street.

ANCIENT AND HONOURABLE ARTILLERY COMPANY, EXCHANGE PLACE, PROVIDENCE, OCTOBER 2, 1903, PHOTO BY E. CHICKERING & CO.

The photographer positioned himself near Providence City Hall to get this view of the Color Guard of the First Light Infantry of Rhode Island and the Ancient and Honourable Artillery Company of London marching around Exchange Place. The local infantry, whose clubhouse was Infantry Hall on South Main Street, had sponsored a visit to the city by the British company and held this parade in their honor. Afterwards the visitors and their guests took a ride on the steamer *Mount Hope* to attend a clambake at Crescent Park. Newspaper accounts mention that the British were unsure how to open clams until the natives demonstrated the technique. In the center of the picture near the Soldiers and Sailors monument, a photographer captures the scene from a different angle.

OLD HOME DAY, FOSTER, 1907

In 1899 New Hampshire Governor Frank West Rollins inaugurated "Old Home Week," a reunion occasion billed as "an opportunity to come back to their old homes and meet once more their old friends and schoolmates." Within a few years Maine, Massachusetts, Vermont, and Rhode Island all followed suit. In the small community of Foster, crowds of residents and returning natives celebrate "Old Home Day," a gathering on the grounds of a historic house. A welcome sign over the doorway encourages people to step inside. To the left, a notice proclaims that cake can be found under the bunting.

HUMAN FLAG, JUNE 3, 1916

Thousands of people watched at Exchange Place as 50,000 participants marched during Providence's six-and-a-half-hour Preparedness Day parade, in anticipation of the U.S. entry into World War I. On the steps of Providence City Hall, over 1,500 school girls dressed in red, white, and blue created a "living flag." Civil War veterans who were members of the Grand Army of the Republic acted as guards, sitting on either side of the flag. At one point the schoolchildren sang the "Star Spangled Banner."

In the late nineteenth century and early twentieth century, "living flags" appeared in cities around the country for ceremonies honoring Civil War veterans, heroes such as the Wright Brothers, and presidents. They became a featured part of celebrations marking civic anniversaries, "Old Home Weeks," and, as shown here, pre–World War I Preparedness Day rallies.

SELLING WAR STAMPS, MARKET SQUARE, PROVIDENCE, 1917–1918

In Market Square, a smiling volunteer sits in the window of a "Liberty Bell" booth fashioned from fabric, ready to sell war saving stamps that helped finance the First World War. They sold for 25 cents to 5 dollars and were collected in booklets; when full the owner received a war bond. "Proclaim Liberty Unto All Inhabitants" was printed around the top of these bells. Close to 23,000 Rhode Island men served in the Armed forces during World War I. On the home front, sales of war saving stamps and Liberty Bonds helped finance the war.

In Market Square, a woman in a fur-collared coat stands nearby selling flowers from her tray. A sign attached to the railing behind her, "Do Not Spit on the Sidewalks, $20.00 fine" was part of a public health campaign.

CITY HALL, PROVIDENCE, 1917–1918

Another bell for selling Liberty bonds is seen near the steps of Providence City Hall, where pedestrians rush past its multiple windows. A billboard behind it says, "Do it Again, Buy Your Liberty Bonds To-day."

LOOKING NORTH ON NORTH MAIN STREET, PROVIDENCE, JULY 4, c. 1874, STEREOGRAPH

Arches as architectural symbols of victory and triumph date back to ancient Rome's Arch of Titus. During the nineteenth century, arches again became a symbol for celebration, a result of the construction of the Arc de Triomphe in Paris, which took over thirty years (1805–1836).

This triumphal arch spanned North Main Street in front of the First Baptist Church. A handwritten caption on the back of this stereograph attributed it to "Packard" without stating his responsibility or exactly what was being celebrated. Dr. Alpheus Spring Packard was a geologist, entomologist, zoologist, and medical doctor who joined the faculty of Brown University in 1878.

On the arch are painted patriotic shields with flags on either column. The name Howard appears on the left shield; the name on the right one is illegible. Round medallions also contain the name Grant—probably the Civil War general Ulysses S. Grant, who was president from 1868 to 1877. Ropes of greenery trim the urn-topped columns and edges of the arch.

In the 1870s, North Main Street was part of the commercial center of town. Once known as Towne Street, this highway ran from Providence to Pawtucket. The silk top hats and fashionable suits worn by the cluster of men on the left side of the arch identify them as successful businessmen. One gentleman walks his dog, while workers in shirt sleeves look out the windows of nearby businesses. On the right in front of the church stand men in work shirts and caps. In the center, a horse-drawn trolley car, like most of the other onlookers, pauses for the photographer. Behind the trolley an American flag hung across the street waves in the breeze.

COTTON CENTENNIAL ARCH, PAWTUCKET, 1890

Spinning wheels, flags, images of spinning wheels, and an engraving of Samuel Slater adorn the top of this arch across Main Street, which commemorated the centennial of cotton manufacturing. Slater, who emigrated from England, established the first successful cotton mill in the United States in Pawtucket. Full-size evergreen trees decorate the base. Shoppers and merchants stop to watch the photographer capture this moment. A boy crosses the trolley tracks carrying bundled kindling, while other boys face the camera. In the distance, buggies and carriages roll down the street.

COTTON CENTENNIAL, PAWTUCKET, 1890

A military reenactment group wearing plumed hats, high boots, and tight-fitting pants, and sabers marches by crowds gathered to see the Cotton Centennial parade. Men lean out upper-story windows and gather on the fire escape of a factory to see the activity. The photographer probably stood on a platform to gain this vantage point over the heads of the spectators.

COTTON CENTENNIAL, MAIN STREET, PAWTUCKET, 1890

Throughout the city of Pawtucket, businesses hung bunting and decorated facades for the Cotton Centennial celebration, during which parades and special events took place. Divisions of marchers pass under draped flags, past spectators lining Pawtucket's main thoroughfare. A marching band playing a tune is followed by men in uniform walking in formation while holding what appears to be a rope attached to a wagon. Rather than watch from street level, a few men have chosen the rooftop of a city building to view the action.

COLUMBUS CELEBRATION, PROVIDENCE, 1892

Two years after the Cotton Centennial, an arch sixty to eighty feet high stands at the head of Westminster Street, near Jackson and Cathedral Square, for the four hundredth anniversary of Columbus's journey to the New World. It dwarfs nearby bunting-draped buildings and the statue of Thomas Arthur Doyle, a former Providence mayor. The original designs, published in the *Providence Journal,* showed an arch covered in vines with a statue of Columbus standing in the center flanked by scale models of the Niña and Pinta, but the actual display is much simpler. American and Spanish flags decorate the Romanesque arch, covered to look like Italian marble, and electric lights in three colors spell "Columbus 1892." At night twenty-six mammoth lights illuminated the area around the temporary structure. Men and boys stand at the base, while a horse-drawn street car goes up the street.

The celebration began at dawn on October 21 with ringing church bells as well as the sounds of cannons and a drum corps. Trains and steamboats brought people in from the suburban areas for the day's events. Over a thousand militia and ten thousand school children participated in the parade. At night a torchlight procession of members of local Catholic parishes walked under the arch.

TWO HUNDRED FIFTIETH ANNIVERSARY OF PAWTUCKET, 1921

A crew of volunteer carpenters, including Mayor Robert A. Kenyon and Captain William McGregor, chairman of the Anniversary Committee, lent a hand to build this arch, with its message "Labors Offering," in honor of the two hundred fiftieth anniversary of the founding of the city. It stood on Main Street (now Roosevelt Avenue) from October 8 through 12, 1921. Electric lights illuminated the arch's "Welcome" sign at night. A policeman standing in the middle of the street behind the arch provides a scale for the size of this undertaking. This photo postcard memorializes the structure long after it was demolished.

These temporary arches only exist in period photographs, but any visitor to Rhode Island can visit a metal arch that spans Atwells Avenue in Providence today. In the center of the city's Italian neighborhood, it's adorned with the Italian symbol of abundance and quality, a pine cone.

Innovative, inventive, and independent Rhode Islanders brought economic success to their state and a tradition of being in the forefront of commercial activity. Brick Market in Newport, and Market House in Providence, were the financial centerpieces for their respective cities. Farmers, tradesmen, and deal makers gathered in and around those distinctive buildings to conduct business. Multistory commercial blocks such as the What Cheer Building soon occupied sites nearby.

Industrial enterprises such as the Gorham Manufacturing Company, which produced silver and jewelry, began operations on the East Side of Providence, later constructing immense factories in other parts of the city. The growth and development of Rhode Island's industries secured the state's position in the world marketplace. Small water-powered factories lined the banks of most of the state's rivers, leading to the creation or expansion of small villages, such as Ashaway, where employees needed housing and services. In Pawtucket, Fales & Jenks and Royal Weaving Company were part of the textile trade, the former supplying factories with machinery and the latter producing finished cloth. In the nineteenth century, Natick Mills, in Natick, was reputed to be the largest cotton manufacturing complex in the world. Costume jewelry began to be manufactured in Providence in tiny shops in what became a huge and profitable endeavor. Rhode Islanders produced more

CHAPTER SIX

INDUSTRIAL AND COMMERCIAL GENIUS
Economic Success and Commercial Activity

than finished products, however; they mined their natural resources, quarrying granite for use in public statues and buildings around the country.

Enclosing a shopping area was a novel concept in early nineteenth century America; across town from today's Providence Place Mall is its earliest New England predecessor, The Arcade, built in 1828. Wood-framed mercantile establishments dominated downtown areas in most towns until merchants constructed big brownstone edifices as evidence of their profitable status. Hotels such as the old Cole's Tavern in Warren and the elaborate Benedict House in Pawtucket became a necessary component in the competition for out-of-state opportunities.

Contributing to the state's affluence was the ability of these industries to move their goods from Rhode Island to the rest of the world. Port towns such as Providence and Bristol had busy waterfronts and harbors, filled with ships loaded with goods produced in the state and with import products.

Behind every commercial success story were the people who labored in the industry. Just like today's enterprises, companies had layers of administrative staff who supervised workers—men, women, and children. The division of labor is as clearly visible in these photographs as the structures in which they worked.

WESTMINSTER AND EDDY STREETS, c. 1864

Except for the woman standing in the doorway of the fourth shop on the right, all of the individuals in this photo of the mercantile section of Providence are men. The watchmaker J. H. Bongartz advertises in his window that he sells at cost. Next door, Nesbitt J. Bowes's larger sign proclaims his business as a boot manufacturer. On the left side, the broad light-colored granite strips define a continuation of the sidewalk and, in the alley, planks lift pedestrians' feet over the mud. A flatbed wagon is parked out front. Down the street is a newer brick building, whereas the shops in the foreground operated out of Colonial-era wooden houses that had been converted for business. Within a few decades, these structures were replaced by multistory commercial blocks. The tracks down the center of Westminster Street are for the horse-drawn street railway lines.

DRY GOODS STORE, EAST GREENWICH, 1876–1879

In the mid-nineteenth century William G. Browning moved to East Greenwich looking for business opportunities and within a few years he bought the dry-goods store, in which he worked. From 1872 to 1879, the commercial enterprise was known as Browning & Fitz, as a result of a partnership with another newcomer, Levi N. Fitz. In 1876 Browning built this brick block to house his expanding business enterprise.

Men stand in both entrances of this dry goods store, while another man crosses a side street. A baby stroller out front indicates a woman with a child is inside.

BRICK MARKET, NEWPORT, c. 1897

The Brick Market was designed by the Colonial architect Peter Harrison and was built between 1760 and 1762, as a market house and public granary. It's still located at the base of Touro and Broadway; today the Newport Historical Society operates it as a museum and gift shop.

Across the top of this photo can be seen the edge of a fabric and wood memorial arch that spans Broadway. The photographer shot the bunting- and flag-draped Brick Market through the arch to frame this street scene. The 45-star American flag seen in this picture became official on July 4, 1896, after Utah was admitted as a state on January 4, 1896, and remained in use until 1908, when Oklahoma became a state on November 16, 1907. A lithograph of George Washington on horseback, probably based on John Faed's painting *Washington Receiving a Salute on the Field of Trenton*, is in the center of the patriotic display. Prints of politicians also decorate the building, suggesting this was an election year. On the upper left is an engraving of William McKinley, president of the United States from 1897 to 1901.

**WHAT CHEER BUILDING, PROVIDENCE, c.1870
STEREOGRAPH IN "THE AMERICAN SCENERY SERIES"**

The name of this block derives from the supposed Narragansett Indian greeting to Roger Williams when he arrived in their lands: "What Cheer, Netop." Built in 1850 on the site of the Manufacturers Hotel, this five-story building was sold to the Rhode Island School of Design in 1957 and eventually was demolished. In this view looking at the What Cheer block on South Main Street, two men stop in the middle of the road to talk while a young boy looks directly at the photographer. A horse-drawn trolley car makes its way on the tracks towards Market Square. According to the signage, businesses in the building included the Connecticut Mutual Life Insurance Co. (L. L. Barnard, General Agent for New England), the Phenix Bank, the Blackstone Canal Bank, the Fourth National Bank, and on the first floor, the American National Bank. Parked on the side of the road, delivery wagons sit while their owners conduct business in the area.

THE ARCADE, PROVIDENCE, c. 1870, STEREOGRAPH BY LEANDER BAKER

Two men caught in conversation seem to be the only customers in The Arcade. However, shadowy shoppers are present; they create a blur as they move past the stores too fast for the slow-exposure camera to capture their figures. In The Arcade, shop windows jut out into the center aisle. On the top floor banners advertise "Alden's Photographs Ambrotypes, porcelains, and copied work." Some of Alden's images appear in this book. In those days, photographers needed natural light to take pictures, and so they chose upper-level studios because of their abundant sunlight. Across the way, another banner proclaims, "ambrotypes and crayons, 6 large pictures only a $1.00." This large picture notice refers to crayon portraits, a photo enhanced with charcoal and other artist materials and suitable for framing. Alden operated a large studio at The Arcade from the late 1860s into the 1870s.

WESTMINSTER STREET VIEW OF THE ARCADE, c. 1870, STEREOGRAPH

James H. Palmer, a merchant in The Arcade, sold this stereograph view of the building. Figures moving too fast for the camera's lens look ghostly walking past the Bon Marché shop next door. At the base of the gaslight in front of The Arcade, a case filled with photographs and a notice proclaiming "dress plaiting" advertise businesses within the establishment. Carriages parked at the curb wait for their owners.

A group of investors built The Arcade in 1828 to encourage economic growth in the mostly residential area of the city. The Greek Revival building was designed by the early-nineteenth-century architects Russell Warren, William Tallman, and James Bucklin. Three stories of shopping stalls allowed customers to browse as they walked through the granite structure on their way to or from Weybosset or Westminster streets.

SPENCER BLOCK, PHENIX, 1871–1873

This four-story building in Phenix, a village in West Warwick, was a shopper's paradise. Most of the town's residents labored in the local cotton factory, but a few enterprising individuals supplied goods and services to those workers. B. Carroll, a milliner, displays hats in her second-floor shop, while next door W. H. Snow works as a merchant and tailor. Two little girls and a dog look at the photographer snapping this shot, perhaps waiting to visit the confectioner down the row. A sign over a center doorway and a bulletin board with samples indicates that the photographer has a studio here. Two men in jackets pose in front of the largest establishment, E. C. Capwell's, a druggist. Beside it on the right, a pair of men lean on the railing in front of the Pawtuxet Valley Shoe Store. A striped pole signifies that a barber occupies the last shop on the right. On the lower level, F. M. and R. F. Carroll sell household goods—crockery, glassware, and tinware—near a wallpaper store, and a person named Richardson does cabinet work. Out front, a young boy stands near a horse-drawn wagon whose owner is most likely shopping. A central water trough for horses topped by a gaslight sits in the center of the unpaved street. The Spencer block burned in 1873.

VIEW AT ASHAWAY LOOKING UP HIGH STREET, c. 1875, STEREOGRAPH IN "THE PEOPLE'S" SERIES

This picture of High Street in Ashaway, a village in Hopkinton, was probably taken from the fishing-line factory of Ashaway Line and Twine Manufacturing Company. On the banks of the Ashaway River an unidentified structure—perhaps a sawmill, judging by the boards stacked on the side of the building—gets power from the water; on the opposite side is the wooden-framed Bethel Manufacturing. A wooden fence on either side of the street protects carriages from falling into the river; wooden steps provide access to the wooden-plank building in the foreground. On the other side of the street a hitching post is visible. A brick mercantile building with two-tone roofing can be seen farther along High Street.

ASHAWAY, c. 1880, PHOTO BY O. LANGWORTHY & CO.

As the stagecoach arrives in downtown Ashaway, men gather on the steps of the Ashaway National Bank, one of two financial institutions in this small Hopkinton village. The bank is visible in the distance in the previous photo. The driver is ready to go, posed with reins in hand. Across the street, a man with a wagon full of barrels turns around to face the camera, while another fellow stands in the middle of the street for inclusion in this street scene. In the late nineteenth century, Ashaway had approximately five hundred residents and a grade school.

BENEDICT HOUSE, PAWTUCKET, MID-1870s, STEREOGRAPH

In this view, snow and ice cover Main and Broad streets in front of the Benedict House hotel, which opened in 1871. Located on the site of a house that belonged to Dr. David Benedict, it was actually named after Stephen Benedict, a president of the People's Bank. Retail shops are on the ground floor, and accommodations on the upper levels. Despite the winter weather, the owner of the corner store has hung out clothing on the corner of the building and placed trunks on the steps to attract shoppers. Behind the hotel, a stable advertises its service with a roof-top sign.

JEWELRY FACTORY, c. 1900, STEREOGRAPH

Men and women work shoulder to shoulder piecing together jewelry in this stereograph produced by the Keystone Company. Supervisors stand nearby watching the activity. The tools of the trade on the bench include lit gas jets for heating metal, containers of water for quick cooling, and tweezers for shaping the pieces. This could have been taken in any one of the many jewelry shops in Providence.

FALES & JENKS MACHINE COMPANY, PAWTUCKET, SEPTEMBER 1881

Located at 118 Dexter Street near Clay Street, the Fales & Jenks Machine Company manufactured machinery for the cotton industry. David G. Fales and Alvin Jenks established the company in Central Falls in 1830 and moved the business to Pawtucket in 1866.

Office workers line up in front of the company's building with its patriotic memorial display after the assassination of President James Garfield in September 1881. In the center of the bull's-eye-style bunting is a picture of the president. Windows, doorways, and even the arch between buildings are wrapped for the occasion, and the arch is marked with a large G in the center.

ROYAL WEAVING COMPANY, PAWTUCKET, 1912
PHOTO BY LEWIS HINE

The Royal Weaving Company manufactured cotton, silk, and worsted fabrics. Young girls tend the threading machines in a work area illuminated by bright sunlight during the day and overhead lights in the evening. In 1908, the photographer Lewis Hine began working for the Child Labor Committee and took pictures of children at work. He found boys and girls engaged in labor instead of being in school.

GORHAM MANUFACTURING COMPANY, PROVIDENCE, c. 1870

Jabez Gorham started the Gorham Manufacturing Company in 1813 to produce silver and jewelry. His son John continued to expand the product line. At this time, the Gorham company occupied all the buildings seen in this photo in the block bounded by Steeple, North Main, and Canal streets. The signs on the various structures proclaim the factory's products as silverware and electroplate. The First Baptist Church is in the background. Next door is W. E. Barrett's chair and wooden ware factory. In the right foreground, men work near barrels in the street and others wait in the doorway. Two men talk near the Gorham Manufacturing Company while delivery wagons line the curbs around the building. In 1889, Gorham moved to a larger plant in the Elmwood section of the city.

WOMEN'S WORK AT GORHAM MANUFACTURING COMPANY, c. 1895

Female employees in the porcelain and silver industries used their knowledge of drawing and painting to do this skilled labor. By the light of a large window, this woman paints a heavy varnish on a piece of silver while surrounded by other projects—vases and tea cups. She's decorated her workspace with charcoal sketches and paintings. A single vase of flowers adorns the window sill, perhaps to be used as a model for her work. She wears sleeve protectors to keep her clothes clean.

PHOTO STUDIO, GORHAM MANUFACTURING COMPANY, c. 1897

Gorham's in-house photo studio took more than 80,000 pictures annually. Company salesmen carried bound books of images with them around the country as they took orders for the products shown in such photos. A woman in an apron studies photographic proofs of photos of silver tankards made at the factory. White sleeve coverings protect her dress from dirt and chemicals. A man in a work shirt looks on. A press sits on the counter and there is an oil can nearby.

MUNITIONS WORK AT GORHAM, c. 1918

In this photograph from a company publication titled Women's Work at Gorham (1918), women stand in a line assembling metal bomb casings while a male supervisor oversees the work. A wooden case of finished casings is next to boxes of other products ready for shipment. During World War I, Gorham manufactured munitions like these to help with the war effort.

NOON HOUR, NATICK MILLS, NATICK, APRIL 17, 1909, ATTRIBUTED TO LEWIS HINE

In this photo labeled by the photographer Lewis Hine, four people leave the office of the Natick Mills complex with their lunch pails in their hands. Five six-story brick mill buildings made this factory, owned by B. B. and R. Knight, one of the largest cotton manufacturers in the world at the time. Hundreds of workers tended the looms and spindles. Women and girls also found employment as office clerks and machine operators. Competition from factories opening up in the South led to the closure of the mills in the 1920s. A fire in 1941 destroyed these buildings.

ATLANTIC FIRE & MARINE INSURANCE CO., WESTMINSTER STREET, PROVIDENCE, c. 1899

A well-dressed woman walks in front of the five-story building at 45 Westminster Street, home to the First National Bank, the Atlantic Fire & Marine Insurance Co., and an architectural firm. Atlantic Fire, incorporated in 1852, issued policies to merchants seeking to insure their goods during shipping. In 1891, the company received total premiums of $3.5 million and paid out losses of $2.5 million; with assets in that year of $250,000, it was one of the largest businesses in the city. The cigar dealers Huntoon & Gorham had the perfect retail location, next door to a building filled with male employees. Near their glass show windows, a boy crosses the street with his hands raised.

WALDORF LUNCH, WESTMINSTER STREET, PROVIDENCE, c. 1930

Downtown workers on their midday break could take advantage of this restaurant in the center of town. This one advertises "Lunches Put up to Take Out" for anyone too busy to take a seat at a table. Upstairs, Henry Dunnell sold stocks and gave investment advice. Next door, Ockel, a clock maker, brags that his shop's watches tell the correct time, and a textile broker, Edward Shaw 2nd, announces that he deals in "cotton goods, print cloths, and yarns."

SMITHFIELD UNION BANK, WOONSOCKET

The Smithfield Union Bank, the oldest financial institution in Woonsocket's Union Village area, operated out of this simple two-story wood structure. Although it could be mistaken for a residence, its function is identified by the placard over the door. Chartered in 1805, the bank kept valuables in the basement. In the 1850s, the business moved to a new building in the main part of Woonsocket.

"NICHOLS AND LANGWORTHY'S MACHINE SHOP," HOPE VALLEY, c. 1876, STEREOGRAPH BY C. SEAVER, JR.

According to the clock tower on the shop, it is 5:20 in the afternoon when a man in a top hat arrives in his carriage at the Langworthy and Company factory in the little village of Hope Valley in Hopkinton. Gardner Nichols and Josiah and Joseph Langworthy manufactured textile machinery at their machine shop, which was founded in 1835. In the late nineteenth century the company also built steam engines for the New York Safety Steam Power Company at this complex. In the middle distance is a lever and pulley system for lifting heavy goods from wagons or for loading items onto wagons. The central tower has several doors with a pulley for lifting materials up to appropriate floors. Visible to the left are spilt-rail fences of this rural farming area.

METAL PRODUCTS CORPORATION BUILDING, PROVIDENCE, 1909

A man prepares to cross the cobblestone street in front of an empty factory building. A sign announces, "This building will be occupied about August 1st by the Metal Products Corporation and the Screw Machine Products Corporation." In 1909 the two companies consolidated their factory operations in this factory on Eddy Street. The Metal Products Corporation made small metal pieces such as jewelers' findings, and the Screw Machine Products Corporation manufactured screws and nuts. Management designed the structure for expansion with the possibility of adding extra floors as needed. Public transportation brought workers to the factory via the railway tracks seen in the street.

RHODE ISLAND GRANITE WORKS, WESTERLY, c. 1876, STEREOGRAPH BY C. SEAVER

The Rhode Island Granite Works, whose business headquarters was the New England Granite Works in Hartford, Connecticut, was one of seven quarries in Westerly that produced stone of various shades. This particular quarry cut fine white granite. Deep in the pit of the quarry, a man stands in the doorway of a log-roofed stone shed. A ladder leans against the walls, providing him with a way to the surface. Men standing on the edge of the quarry look towards the photographer. In the background can be seen the statue *Antietam Soldier*. A man on a ladder closely inspects the carving. In the background are company buildings.

ANTIETAM MEMORIAL STATUE, WESTERLY, c. 1876, STEREOGRAPH IN "THE RHODE ISLAND SERIES"

The statue *Antietam Soldier* was designed by James G. Batterson of Hartford, Connecticut as a memorial to be placed at the Civil War battlefield of Antietam in Maryland. It depicts a Union soldier at ease. With a height of 21.5 feet and a weight of 30 tons, it dwarfs the men and dog on the ground; its base was 23.5 feet high. James Pollette of Westerly sculpted it from a single block of white granite quarried from the Rhode Island Granite Works. It first stood at the Centennial Exposition in Philadelphia in 1876 and was dedicated at the National Cemetery at Antietam in 1880. The barn was used to store other statues made from stone won from the quarry. The nineteenth-century photographer edited out the scaffolding seen in the smaller picture at left.

OFFICE AT THE DIAMOND HILL QUARRY, CUMBERLAND, c. 1880, STEREOGRAPH

At the hitching post in front of this ivy-covered office building stand three employees of the Diamond Hill Quarry. Diamond Hill, a village in Cumberland, was known for its rocky geography and the presence of minerals such as quartz, iron ore, and granite. On the right a man in a wide brimmed straw hat, probably a surveyor, studies his notebook while the middle one stares off in the distance with open notebook in hand. The man on the left with the plaid shirt and bowler hat looks directly at the photographer.

DIAMOND HILL QUARRY, c. 1880, STEREOGRAPH

From the top of a small hill, this photographer captured a workday scene at the Diamond Hill Quarry. Men stop work to face the camera. A flatbed railway car loaded with granite blocks can be seen on the tracks. In the foreground the intersecting lines are cables attached to pulleys for lifting the stones. A long shed on the right is for storage. An immense pile of discarded rock looms behind a building in the rear of the picture. At the time of this picture, approximately fifteen men labored at the quarry; eight appear in this shot.

PROVIDENCE RIVER, c. 1900

This busy harbor scene is evidence of Providence's dominance as a port at the turn of the century. In the early twentieth century, this activity moved to the new State Pier, constructed off Allens Avenue. Two men sit on the deck of a steam-powered tugboat; surrounded by all types of sailing and other vessels. On the center-left, next to the Ryder Bros. Salt Works warehouse, a three-masted ship is tied up at the dock. Beside it, another vessel rides low in the water. In the background is a sign for Hopkins Coal Pier.

Not everyone worked for a large business entity; some companies had only a few employees or were family owned and operated. For instance, the marine industries of fishing and shellfishing operated as small ventures such as the Narragansett Bay Oyster Company. Individual fishermen owned boats that operated out of Rhode Island's ports and smaller coastline harbors to supply the marketplace with fresh seafood.

Some merchants continued to operate as they always had—from storefronts and out of the backs of wagons carrying their goods around the countryside, towns, and cities. It was a tenuous existence, and their economic stability was entirely dependent on their

CHAPTER SEVEN

EARNING A LIVING
Making Ends Meet

customers' well-being. Every town relied on these individual enterprises for goods and services. The Gold Medal Creamery sold its products to grocers, who in turn sold to housewives.

Others worked as public and civil servants: men and women who worked in state-run academic institutions teaching students as well as those who administered state facilities such as the Rhode Island State Prison.

These photographs show a layered economy with businesses such as the Metropolitan French Cleaners and Dyers catering to a well-off clientele and G. W. Easterbrooks Saddlery catering to the needs of the middle-class for harnesses. The average man had his hair cut at Allen's, while successful business men and those who considered themselves of that ilk sought out the services of Clough's carpeted establishment. Those too poor to afford luxuries could find what they needed at Burnett S. W. Bragunn's Curiosity Shop, a pawnshop and reseller of secondhand goods.

Today it is difficult to locate a small, family-run grocery store, but most of the mercantile and commercial services represented here still exist, albeit in different forms. Rhode Island continues to have a diverse economy. It's not the type of businesses that have changed, but the way everyone does their work. Teachers still instruct, shopkeepers sell goods, and families can still work together to ensure their financial success.

138 PREPARING OYSTERS FOR SHIPMENT,
NARRAGANSETT BAY OYSTER CO.,
85 GANO STREET, PROVIDENCE, 1908,
PHOTO BY WILLIAM MILLS

At one time Providence Harbor supported a healthy shellfishing industry, and the photographer William Mills captured this scene of men washing, sorting, and packing oysters for shipment from a Providence company. The rectangular box prominently displayed in the center is clearly a prop to advertise the company. To its left a man hammers shut a tub of oysters. Behind the box a supervisor appears to be studying a packing list. In the background two workers, one an African American man, douse recently harvested shells with water and lay them out in trays. On the far wall, a calendar marks the month and year: November 1908.

PICTURING RHODE ISLAND EARNING A LIVING

GOLD MEDAL CREAMERY, PROVIDENCE, c. 1900

Under this prominent sign for W. W. Whipple Company, the merchants Dillon & Douglass and the Gold Medal Creamery shared space in this building on Canal Street. The sign on the wagon indicates that the creamery supplied butter, lard, cheese, and poultry from their Providence branch office. The company's main headquarters were in Connecticut. Two men stand near the entrance loading products from the cold-storage area in the basement.

BURNETT S. W. BRAGUNN'S CURIOSITY SHOP, SOUTH MAIN STREET, PROVIDENCE, c. 1890

This unusual shop on the waterfront sold an eclectic mix of services and goods for mariners. Customers could buy second-hand clothing, tools, boats, and boat hardware, purchase railroad tickets for travel, or store their furniture "for fifty cents a week." A crude painting of Jack the Ripper, complete with a bloody knife, adorns the facade. On the far right of the building is a collection of advertising symbols for illiterate patrons—an anchor, a set of oarlocks, and a trio of oars. The universal sign for a pawnshop (a draw for sailors and others in need of cash), three balls or spheres, is prominently displayed on a small awning. The Curiosity Shop was demolished in about 1890.

NURSERY, NASONVILLE, 1880s, STEREOGRAPH BY G. P. LOVELL

A man in overalls, boots, and a wide-brimmed hat stands in the doorway of this unusual building, with its wall of windows on the first floor. Saplings grow in a row in the backyard, their roots protected by wooden frames. This appears to be a greenhouse in the little village of Nasonville, located in the town of Burrillville. At the time of this photo, approximately a hundred people lived in this community. It had just two stores and one textile mill.

SPRAYING THE ORCHARDS AT THE RHODE ISLAND COLLEGE OF AGRICULTURE AND MECHANICAL ARTS, KINGSTON, 1908

This metal-wheeled horse-drawn wagon enabled agricultural students at the Rhode Island College of Agriculture and Mechanic Arts, now the University of Rhode Island, to transport a tank of pesticide. One man checks the compressor at the rear of the wagon. Snaking behind him along the ground is a hose connected to the long handled sprayer held by the man in the foreground.

142 RHODE ISLAND NORMAL SCHOOL, PROVIDENCE, c. 1910

The Rhode Island Normal School began training teachers in 1854; it is now called Rhode Island College. A female instructor stands in front of a blackboard in a wood-working class. In the center, a young man and an older woman hold a saw while the rest of the students work on their projects.

METROPOLITAN FRENCH CLEANERS & FANCY DYERS, NEWPORT, c. 1930

In an era when employees wore uniforms identifying their trade, these delivery men pose proudly, attired in high boots, long buttoned jackets, and visored hats. Their garments and specially marked vehicles referring to the "French" cleaning method reflected the company's commitment to quality services catering to Newport's affluent community. A dry cleaner in Paris in the 1840s first used effective but highly flammable petroleum-based chemicals to remove stains from woolens and other textiles that could not be laundered. By the time of this photo in the 1930s, the "French" process used a nonflammable fluid.

ICE HARVESTING, PROBABLY GREEN POND, NEWPORT, c. 1890

Planks have been laid down to outline the area of ice to be harvested from Green Pond and to provide a surface for workers to stand on. Near the planks pairs of workers use six-foot-long saws to cut the ice into blocks. Then workers near the storage houses use long-handled picks to move the blocks into the buildings to be packed in sawdust. The windowed structure on the far right probably sheltered men during breaks. In the late nineteenth century, Frederick Tudor, known as the "Ice King," developed a market for New England ice in markets around the world. In 1886, American men harvested over 25 million tons of frozen water.

"RICHMOND SAW MILL", EXETER, c. 1920

Ernest Gardner, standing on the left, and his log man, Frank Johnson, stand near their sawmill, which has produced the large mound of sawdust in the background. To their right, logs from area forests are ready to be sawed into planks. The positioning of the two men in this photo appears to indicate that Johnson would lift a trunk into place while Gardner kept it steady as it passed the blade.

B. R CHILDS'S HARNESS SHOP, WARREN, c. 1865, STEREOGRAPH BY A. G. ELDREDGE

The photographer captured two men in vests and work shirts posed in the left-hand doorway of this shop. Both are busy tooling leather harness pieces. In the other opening a man, probably the owner, a Mr. Childs, wearing a jacket, vest and a high silk hat, stands with his hands gripping his coat lapels. Hung beside him are sample wares. On the sign, Childs advertised his services as a harness and trunk maker.

G. W. EASTERBROOKS SADDLERY, PAWTUCKET, c. 1878

Giles W. Easterbrooks and Adam Lassard stand in front of their store with rolled-up shirtsleeves and wearing leather work aprons. A horse blanket hangs on either side of the doorway. Signs proclaim they sell "horse clothing" and "saddlery goods." A collar for a draft horse collar hangs to their right, and various tools and equipment are on display in the store windows. Easterbrooks later served as the mayor of Pawtucket (1911–1918).

W. ALLEN'S SHOP, THAMES STREET, NEWPORT, c. 1889

The striped poles framing the doorway and at the corner of the building, as well as the man's long coat, identify this business as a barbershop. In city directories, William Allen reported his occupation as a hairdresser. This one-person enterprise offered the average man a simple haircut and shave. A sign on the lower right-hand side states the building is for sale and gives the name of the realtor, G. V. Wilbur.

CLOUGH & CO., HAIR DRESSING ROOMS, 97 WEYBOSSET STREET, PROVIDENCE, c. 1882, STEREOGRAPH

Many twenty-first-century hair salons offer clients extra amenities and atmosphere, but few can compare to the finest establishments of the late nineteenth century. In 1882, Joseph Clough, an Englishman, opened this hairdressing establishment, with an attached parlor for men. It featured wall frescoes, an upright piano, a water fountain, and a fish tank filled with shells and goldfish. The center table contained a cologne fountain, two cases of stuffed birds, and a music box. The ten barber's chairs were designed and patented by Clough. He offered hair preparations as well as hot and cold baths. His elaborately carpeted and chandeliered facilities with a gaslight at each work station and live music made visiting the salon a total experience.

ROBERT R. CARR'S MEAT AND VEGETABLE WAGON, 1870–1872, STEREOGRAPH BY THEODORE F. CHASE

In the nineteenth century, shopping for basic goods wasn't a matter of driving down to the local supermarket. Robert R. Carr sold meat and vegetables directly to his customers from the back of his wagon. At the rear of the wagon, Carr turns toward the cameraman as he sharpens his knife, getting ready to carve some meat. He is shown here posed with his customer, a housewife, a few children, and his helper in an apron. In the age before refrigeration, it's unclear from this picture how Carr kept his products from spoiling on this summer's day.

TANNER STREET, NEWPORT, 1875, PHOTO BY J. A. WILLIAMS

The proud owner of this store posed in the winter for a photograph wearing a fur-trimmed stovepipe hat and his apron under an overcoat. In the open store display, ducks, rabbits, and hogs are visible while parts of other animals hang from meat hooks on the exterior of the building. One of the hog carcasses leans on the edge of the brick-front building. Stacked canned goods, a clay storage jug, and what looks like pies create a tempting window display. The shopkeeper's pants stop above the ankles, perhaps to keep them clean while he is butchering meat. The elderly man in the rocking chair on the left wears a long apron and a felt bowler. Tanner Street later was named West Broadway; in 1994, the street was named Marcus Wheatland Boulevard, in honor of a prominent African American physician in Newport. No buildings from this era are still standing in this part of Newport.

ARTHUR JEFFERSON ("JUMBO"), BROWN UNIVERSITY, c. 1885, PHOTO BY THE HORTON BROTHERS

Students at Brown University purchased food from individuals who established businesses on campus. In 1884, Arthur Jefferson bought his franchise for five dollars from another man, and also acquired the previous owner's nickname, "Jumbo." Snappily dressed in a full-crowned hat, overcoat, and suit, Jefferson would carry baskets of fruit, baked goods, and roasted peanuts around campus. Eventually the university gave him room in the basement of University Hall to use as a food shop. He was such a fixture on campus that Brown featured him in a c.1885 collection of photos of the school.

150 MRS. YOUNG'S GIFT SHOP, ANGELL STREET, PROVIDENCE, c. 1899

When Mrs. Marian Young opened her shop in the late nineteenth century, it was only the second gift shop of its kind in the country; the other was in Boston. Items on display include fancy tea cups, vases, books, prints, and unique needlework designs. As a mother and a daughter enter the shop, a sales clerk stands ready with a ledger and a pen. Mrs. Young shows a client a print while another saleswoman consults with a customer near the window on the right. During the thirty-five years that Young ran her store, this neighborhood, adjacent to Brown University, was a mix of dwellings, small shops, and university buildings. Young retired in 1933.

SOUTH MAIN STREET, PROVIDENCE, 1860s

John B. Chace and one of his sons operated this grocery in the mid-nineteenth century. By the time this picture was taken, in the 1860s, the elder Chace was in his seventies, so he cannot be one of the two men in this photo, since both men are much younger. Baskets full of produce, casks, and jugs line the front of the shop, and tinned goods are visible in the windows.

75 WESTMINSTER STREET, PROVIDENCE, BEFORE 1890, PHOTO BY H. Q. MORTON

In cities and towns around the state, the main streets were lined with clusters of stores, offering customers an opportunity to window-shop. On this corner of Westminster Street, a clerk stares out the window of C. Robert Linke's store, where watches, jewelry, and spectacles were sold. Notice the large pair of glasses over the doorway. Upstairs, John Stott, a hair cutter, had a room and the Rhode Island Exchange for Woman's Work had its salesroom for women's handiwork. On the other side of the entrance, James Allen advertised furnishings and rugs. A bankruptcy sale at the pottery, glass, and tinware shop hints at the financial realities faced by some merchants.

WILLIAM K. TOOLE HARDWARE, PAWTUCKET, 1914

Employees gathered in the front of the store for this photograph of Toole Hardware, once located at 178–180 Main Street. The youngest employee, Rock Martin, is in the picture. Founded 1901, the store sold an assortment of goods, from Goodyear and Ajax tires to household appliances such as gas and electric lights. A row of fans sit on top of display shelves on the right. In the glass cases are boxes of light bulbs and a tea set.

THE BEE HIVE, THAMES STREET, NEWPORT, 1934–1935

A German immigrant, Louis Hess, opened his dry-goods store in 1882, founding a family business that lasted well into the twentieth century. By the time of this photo, Hess and Co., Inc., called their women's dress shop The Bee Hive and showed their wares in two-story-high Art Deco display windows. Stockings are draped over racks on the first floor with dresses hanging in the upstairs windows. The proprietor proudly stands in the entryway to the store as customers pass by.

EARNING A LIVING   PICTURING RHODE ISLAND

154 T. M. MORRIS'S, THAMES STREET, POSSIBLY BRISTOL, c. 1900

Expensive molded wooden letters proclaim T. M. Morris's saloon as the spot to buy well-known Rhode Island beers such as Hanley's Peerless Ale and the Providence Brewing Co.'s Bohemian Beer. Incorporated in 1891, the James Hanley Brewing Co., located on the corner of Fountain and Jackson streets, was one of the oldest brewers in the state. Hanley employed German immigrants in his brewery.

Two bartenders stand in the doorway of the saloon wearing clean white coats and aprons. Inside, another stands behind the bar, underneath bunting-wrapped poles, pouring liquor and mixing drinks for the camera. Towels hang below the bar for men to wipe their mouths, and there are spittoons on the floor. Two small signs overhead advertise Narragansett lager, ales, and porters, as well as Holter's lager and Garrick's rye. Reflected in the mirrors are the establishment's wallpaper and the camera's flash.

NEWPORT WATERWORKS, WEST MARLBOROUGH STREET, NEWPORT, c. 1884

The employees of the Newport Waterworks pose in front of their main office, tools in hand. A young boy in the front row and two men behind him hold mallets while others sit with a giant pair of pliers in their laps. Other men hold hammers and tongs. The grime on their faces and clothes suggest this was taken after work. The privately owned Newport Waterworks supplied Newport with water from Easton's Pond. At the turn of the nineteenth century, frequent outbreaks of typhoid in the city were traced to the water quality. Note Holloway's Photo Parlor in the background.

STATE PRISON, CRANSTON, c. 1880

In the prison yard at the state prison at Howard, a village in Cranston, a man, probably the warden, watches his dog, which seems to be watching the photographer. Behind them, a small cow grazes. This stone complex with its octagonal central structure replaced the old state prison in Providence in 1878. This area is currently under development.

POSTAL TELEGRAPH AND CABLE OFFICE, THAMES STREET, NEWPORT, c. 1900

These five boys proudly pose in their official uniforms, with two of the bicycles they used for delivering telegrams. Their supervisors stand next to them, the two on the right themselves barely out of their teenage years. Delivering telegrams was clean work for these young laborers—in this era, their peers often found employment in the mills.

OLD POST OFFICE, DAVISVILLE, c. 1890

A mailman for R.F.D. no. 1 (rural free delivery, route no. 1) stands next to his horse-drawn mail carriage near the local post office. The village of Davisville had fewer than one hundred residents at the time of this photo. Davisville was a small community on the Stonington & Providence Railroad, until the Navy built a facility there during World War II for manufacturing Quonset huts, a type of modular, all-purpose military building.

TRAP-FISHING CREW, NEWPORT, MAY 1920

This crew looks relaxed before the camera, dressed in their work clothes—loose shirts, caps, and rubber boots. These men and many others fished out of Rhode Island ports and harbors such as Newport. They spent weeks out at sea catching fish using traps that allowed the fish to swim in but not out again. The fish were immediately put on ice in the hold.

TRAP-FISHING CREW, NEWPORT, MAY 1920

At the dock, the men unload the hold. The man on board empties the bulkhead, swinging one bucket of fish at a time to the dock. Another shovels ice to keep the catch cold, and still other men put hoops on the wooden barrels to be used for storage, while the fellow on the left leans on a hand truck, waiting to cart away the full load.

In the last years of the nineteenth century and the early years of the twentieth, public building projects all over the state reshaped Rhode Island. Bridges, buildings, and roadways became iconographic expressions of how Rhode Islanders felt about their future: confident. Population was still increasing; business was booming and the economy was growing.

The Red Bridge connecting Providence's East Side to East Providence was a significant project. The original was a toll bridge known as the Central Bridge, a drawbridge that had been in operation since the eighteenth century. The expanded capacity of the new, improved drawbridge reflected the volume of traffic between the two communities by the 1890s. It would remain in place until the 1970s, when instead of a trussed bridge it became a wide roadway.

Two years later, an extension to the bridge near Weybosset Street, which connected the East Side to downtown Providence, was built with wooden pilings. The access road between the two areas was crammed with vehicles and pedestrians, and more travel space was required.

Anyone driving into Rhode Island from the north on Route 95 can see the State House, its marble dome visible for miles in all directions from its location on Smith Hill. A bustling business

CHAPTER EIGHT

BUILDING RHODE ISLAND
A Century of Change

environment needed a political edifice to match the ambitions of its leaders. The old state house on Benefit Street no longer fit the "new" Rhode Island. This replacement took six years to build.

The junction of Weybosset and Westminster streets was a significant land feature. The V-shaped intersection was the gateway to the original downtown residential area, which in the nineteenth century became an important commercial district. On that spot sat first a house, then the Whitman Block, and now the Turk's Head Building. Harking back to the neighborhood's origins, a marble Turk's head adorns the prow of this building, an allusion to the figurehead that supposedly marked the front of Jacob Whitman's dwelling.

Growing communities need updated services. In the late 1890s, a new sewer system at Field's Point accommodated the expansion of Rhode Island's populous communities. An increased need for water led the state to construct the Scituate Reservoir to supply water to Providence and the surrounding communities.

Probably the most dramatic change was the building of the Interstate Highway System in the 1960s. Whole neighborhoods in towns along its route disappeared, demolished by the wrecking ball, and were replaced by miles of smooth asphalt. Plans were approved for a new bridge across the East Passage of Narragansett Bay to do away with the old ferry system.

In the twentieth century, Newport, like Providence, experienced rapid changes. The city sought a way to encourage tourism in the wake of the departure of the U.S. Navy's resident destroyer fleet, along with all the regular sailors and their dependents out of the area, and the concomitant loss of related economic activity. In the late 1960s, whole neighborhoods and commercial districts along Thames Street were demolished to create America's Cup Boulevard and a series of new shopping districts. The Naval War College stayed in Newport and greatly expanded.

North, south, east, and west, Rhode Island has been reinvented as a modern state while retaining a flavor of the old. A resident from 1850 might immediately feel at home and recognize certain neighborhoods and villages, but might also be overwhelmed by unrecognizable change just a few blocks away. In these pictures you can follow the metamorphosis of Rhode Island.

CENTRAL BRIDGE CONSTRUCTION, PROVIDENCE, c. 1895

A schoolboy in a suit, tie, and cap sits on the end of the Waterman Street side of the Central Bridge. Below him, workmen make adjustments to a support resting on stone pilings, their coats draped over the metal. Up on the bridge is a wheelbarrow; in the background, on the right, a group of men are working. The gatehouse is on the right. This 1895 span, named the Central Bridge, was commonly known as the Red Bridge after the original span which was built in 1793.

A VIEW OF THE SEEKONK RIVER, c. 1890

Three bridges spanned the Seekonk River in the late nineteenth century: the Central Bridge (Red Bridge), the Washington Bridge, and a railroad bridge. This span is likely the railroad bridge, linking East Providence and Providence. Lights illuminate the bridge at night, warning sailors of its location. A wooden house at the base of the bridge is probably for the drawbridge operator. In the foreground are small boathouses that were built out on the river on gravel-covered points of land. On the shore small skiffs are pulled up onto the grassy beach. Note the small covered bridge in the background on the right. The clubhouse for the Narragansett Boat Club sits on a small piece of land in the river.

RED BRIDGE, BEFORE 1895

The third Red Bridge was built over the Seekonk River in 1872 to connect East Providence to Waterman Street on Providence's East Side. It was replaced in 1895 by the Central Bridge. A horse and wagon make their way toward the Providence side of the river. Across the river, the factory for the American Ship Windlass Company is identified by the sign on its roof.

CONSTRUCTION OF THE CENTRAL BRIDGE, MAY 11, 1895

It takes a team of eight men to hoist a stone block from the flatbed railway car on the pier to their boat. These blocks were for the base of the new Central Bridge. On the pier another worker pulls a rope attached to the pulley, while below him a man stands next to a coal-fired engine. In the distance are the houses of the East Side and the Manville Covering Company's sign, "Steam Pipe and Boiler Covering."

RED BRIDGE GATEHOUSE, MAY 29, 1895

The gatekeeper, in a uniform consisting of a double-breasted coat and a high-crowned cap, poses with another man next to the brick home for the keeper of the drawbridge. This dwelling was part of the 1870–1873 renovation of the original bridge. Located on the west side of the Seekonk River, this building is now the Gatehouse Restaurant.

CENTRAL BRIDGE, 1950

As welders work in the foreground, other men wearing hats with upturned brims and tools in hand stop to pose for the photographer. In the center, a man in a delivery uniform also looks at the camera. Near him a supervisor in a felt hat and a long coat inspects the metal surface. Originally built in 1895, the bridge was closed for repairs, as seen here, in 1950. It was demolished in 1976.

FIELD'S POINT, c. 1896

Men stand on the cross beams of a new sewage system for the city of Providence at Field's Point, a peninsula on the western bank of the Providence River. On the right, a man stands on material in a flatbed railroad car. In the background steam engines rest on platforms over the trench. In the next photo men operate a drilling machine.

Field's Point, first a sanitarium then a shore resort, became part of the city's plans to expand shipping operations through harbor improvements in the early twentieth century. A municipal wharf constructed along Allen's Avenue is still used today.

Weybosset Bridge, May 3, 1897

In the late 1890s, Weybosset Bridge, which connected the East Side to downtown Providence, underwent changes to widen it and close in more of the river in front of the Washington Buildings. Torn-up trolley tracks and cobblestones indicate the original roadway.

Men with their backs to the camera watch a fellow worker climb to the top of a piece of machinery while other men in suits supervise the activity. Near the equipment, laborers dig up the street. In the center, trolley cars make their way towards downtown. The Union Passenger Depot is on the right, and the shops and warehouses in the Market Square and Canal Street area are on the left.

WEYBOSSET BRIDGE, c.1897

Two men in overalls and hats and a young man in a jacket and cap walk precariously on logs below street level in the construction area. Wooden pilings that supported the original bridge are visible underneath the vertical planks. A metal pulley bisects the photograph, obscuring the first man's face.

WORK ON THE WEYBOSSET BRIDGE, 1897

A laborer in hip boots and rolled-up shirtsleeves stands in the swirling water of the river while he works near a large pipe. Both the rope anchored to the log next to him and the one he's holding are part of the digging and dredging being done by hand in the river. His shovel is on the pile behind him.

WEYBOSSET BRIDGE, 1897

In this view of the Crawford Street Bridge, the widening of Weybosset Bridge is almost complete. Laborers work in groups laying trolley tracks in the center of the cobblestone surface. On the left, the warehouses along South Water Street were torn down in 1930 and the area made into a parking lot. Today some of that area is a park.

BUILDING THE RHODE ISLAND STATE HOUSE, c. 1896

The architectural firm of McKim, Mead & White of New York won the competition to design the new Rhode Island State House. It was built on a hill, once known as the Jefferson Plain, near Smith Hill. The site overlooked the city center of Providence. Ground-breaking took place on September 16, 1895, and the cornerstone was laid on October 15, 1896.

Swarms of men work lay the brick foundations of the State House domes, surrounded by piles of bricks and wooden barrels. In the foreground men face the camera with wooden brick carriers on their shoulders. In the background a wooden platform holds equipment. To the far left three men in suits supervise the construction.

THE STATE HOUSE, FEBRUARY 9, 1897

In this view, the two wings of the building are under construction. Stacks of marble blocks surround the steel-framed structure. Cranes and pulleys hoist the stone into place. A shed sits to the left of the site. Wooden beams and snow litter the yard.

STATE HOUSE UNDER CONSTRUCTION, c. 1897

This view, probably taken from the Washington Buildings, looks over the rooftops of downtown Providence past the rail yards to the partially built State House and Smith Hill. An American flag atop the frame waves in the breeze. On the right is Canal Street, with its brick buildings and traffic, and the Charles Street neighborhood can be seen in the distance.

STATE HOUSE, NOVEMBER 2, 1899

Scaffolding provides platforms for the men working on the finishing touches on the dome—50 feet in diameter and 149 feet high—and second-floor balcony. Wide wooden work areas stretch along the first floor. In this view, from Smith Street, the steps are not yet in place. State officials moved in on January 1, 1901; landscaping and terraces were completed three and a half years later.

STATE HOUSE, 1936

From 1854 to 1900, Providence and Newport had alternated as state capital, but once the State House was finally completed, in 1900, Providence became the only capital of the state.

Two women walk down the brick pathway on the front of the State House. Behind them people are on the steps and the walkway along the bottom of the terrace provide a sense of the size and scale of the building. The dome on the right is topped by the Rhode Island state flag and the one on the left by the American flag. Topping the center dome is the statue of the "Independent Man," a symbol of the state. Across the pediment of the entrance is the motto "To Hold Forth a Lively Experiment," a reference to the words of Roger Williams, the founder of the colony, and language in the charter given Williams by King Charles II.

INTERSECTION OF WEYBOSSET AND WESTMINSTER STREETS, c. 1850, REVERSED DAGUERREOTYPE

D. H. Braman, wholesale dealer in foreign and domestic fruits and groceries, displays barrels and boxes of goods on the steps of his store. A sign on the Westminster Street side of the shop advertises his wares: oranges, lemons, figs, raisins, pickles, nuts, cigars, and tobacco. He obtained them from the import trade ships that came to the Providence Harbor. In 1750, a Jacob Whitman constructed a house on this site. Sometime in the early nineteenth century Whitman obtained a ship's figurehead of a Turk's head and hung it on his house, giving a name to the neighborhood—Turk's Head. In 1828, this three-story brick warehouse opened and was named Whitman's Block after the original resident.

TURK'S HEAD, c. 1900

People wearing winter coats walk across the wide intersection of Weybosset and Westminster streets. In this photograph, the Whitman Block is now home to a wide variety of business offices and factories such as "A. A. White Co., Stencils" on the third floor. On the second floor, A. Goff sells real estate, mortgages and insurance; down the hall is a monument vendor. A sign on the front of the building tells travelers they can book a four-and-a-half-day trip to Florida for $41.30 from an unidentified agent. The ground-floor central entrance is that of the coal seller Robert L. Smith and Company. Busy commercial Westminster Street is visible on the right.

PICTURING RHODE ISLAND BUILDING RHODE ISLAND

CONSTRUCTION OF TURK'S HEAD BUILDING, c. 1913

Men dig with picks and shovels in the remains of the basement of the Whitman Block. Horse-drawn wagons cart away debris, climbing the ramp to street level. A coal-fired stove dominates the foreground, while another on the left side powers a pile driver. A crowd of spectators has gathered at the construction site to watch the action, just as at any construction site today. In the background are the Tribune Building and the Industrial Trust Company.

TURK'S HEAD BUILDING, c. 1913

A photographer snapped a picture of the newly completed Turk's Head Building from a window in the nearby Washington Row. At the time, this seventeen-floor triangular office building of limestone and granite was the tallest in the city. The Turk's Head commemorates the original masthead said to have decorated the exterior of Jacob Whitman's house in the early nineteenth century.

BUILDING THE SCITUATE RESERVOIR, 1921

Concerned about the health and adequacy of the city's water supply, the Providence City Council voted to create a reservoir in Scituate by damming the Pawtuxet River at the village of Kent. The upriver villages of Richmond, South Scituate, and Ashland became submerged when the reservoir started to fill. This reservoir still supplies water to Providence residents.

A man smoking a cigarette drives a bulldozer, while his supervisor, in a straw hat, watches.

DIGGING THE RESERVOIR, DECEMBER 1, 1921

Work on the reservoir began in 1915 and wasn't completed until September 30, 1926. A man drives a horse-drawn wagon full of dirt away from the construction site. Behind him, a man operates a steam shovel and loads up another wagon in a long train of carts waiting to be filled. On the top right, two wagons can be seen leaving the area. In the background, another piece of steam-powered equipment digs.

AERIAL VIEW OF THE NEWPORT BRIDGE UNDER CONSTRUCTION, 1969

Planning for the Newport Bridge (named the Clairborne Pell Bridge in 1997 in honor of the longest-serving senator in Rhode Island history) to span the East Passage of Narragansett Bay and connect Newport to Jamestown, began in 1944, but actual construction couldn't start until Rhode Island citizens voted in a referendum to fund the project. It took two tries, but state residents finally ratified it in 1965. Work on the 2.13-mile-long bridge began in 1968. Here, small craft pass underneath the skeletal framework of the bridge.

NEWPORT BRIDGE UNDER CONSTRUCTION, 1969

Eight men in heavy winter clothing lay the deck of the Newport Bridge. A man standing next to a pair of saw horses cuts wood to make molds for pouring the concrete blocks. Each block was seven and a half inches thick.

BUILDING RHODE ISLAND **PICTURING RHODE ISLAND**

BAY VIEW OF THE NEWPORT BRIDGE, 1969

The Rhode Island Turnpike and Bridge Authority oversaw the entire construction process, from the divers who cut the piles underwater to the floating cranes used to lift prefabricated pieces of the deck into place.

THAMES STREET, NEWPORT, c. 1900

On a wet and wintry afternoon men walk along Thames Street while horse-drawn hacks wait at the curb for their owners to return from shopping. On the right, the Brick Market building is occupied by the Old City Hall Novel Shop. A sign in the window advertises that they carry baseball supplies. Next door is the Great Atlantic & Pacific Tea Co., while across the street is the Hall & Lyon Apothecary. Narrow Thames Street was known for its mix of Colonial and mid-nineteenth-century buildings and mercantile businesses.

CONSTRUCTION OF AMERICA'S CUP BOULEVARD, MARCH 1967

A policeman stands at the corner near the Newport Youth Center as a group of men watches the demolition of the Boston Store and Eddy's Market. In the 1960s, Newport, in an effort to attract tourists to the area, tore down many of the businesses and bars in the Thames Street neighborhood to improve the appearance and reputation of the area once popular with Navy enlisted men. The end result is America's Cup Boulevard and a collection of shops known as Brick Market Place.

AERIAL VIEW OF I-95 CONSTRUCTION c. 1960

Automobiles still travel on city streets in the area designated for the interstate. A crane and backhoe are in the center of the construction. The division of Providence into two parts on either side of the highway can be clearly seen in this photograph, looking north. Neighborhoods on the left side of the picture experienced economic hardship because the highway cut them off from downtown.

VIEW NORTH, c. 1960

An engineer stands in the middle of what will become I-95. All the surrounding buildings were demolished to create an open lot of land. It provided convenient parking for downtown workers until highway construction began. The towers to the right identify the Cathedral of Saints Peter and Paul in Cathedral Square.

AERIAL VIEW, c. 1965

In this bird's-eye view of the nearly finished highway, looking north, the line of demarcation between residential and commercial Providence is clear. On the right, factories, apartment complexes, and mercantile industrial sites are evident from their parking lots full of cars. To the left are residential neighborhoods full of triple-decker frame buildings. In the right-hand corner of this photo can be seen downtown Providence, the State House, and Kennedy Plaza, near the Industrial Trust Tower.

VIEW OF I-95, 2006, PHOTO BY KEN CARLSON

Nearly fifty years after the completion of the highway, cars travel north and south on I-95 in the spot where the engineer stood in the earlier picture. The cathedral's towers are still visible on the right. The photographer stood on an overpass and faced north to take this picture.

Abbot Park (Providence), 53, 98
Acorn Street (Providence), 30
Akerman's Blank Book Manufactory
    (Providence), 17
Alden (photographer), 121
Allen, James K., 98
Allen, William, 147
Allen's Avenue, 167
Allenton, 40
American National Bank, 120
American Ship Windlass Company, 164
American Steamboat Company, 46, 87
American Supply Company (Providence), 9
America's Cup Boulevard (Newport), 179
Amusement Parks.
    see Parks and Amusement Parks
Ancient and Honorable Artillery Company, 108
Angell Street (Providence), 150
Antietam Memorial Statue, 133
Apponaug (Warwick), 63, 83
Arcade (Providence), 121
Arnold, Thomas W., 48
Arnold Family (Allenton), 40
Arsenal, Providence Marine Corps of Artillery,
    24, 25
Ashaway, Hopkinton, 123
Ashaway Line and Twine Manufacturing
    Company, 123
Ashaway National Bank, 123
Atlantic Building (Providence), 18
Atlantic Fire & Marine Insurance Co., 130
Atwells Avenue (Providence), 103

Banigan Building (Providence), 18
Barnard, L.L., 120
Barrett, W.E., 127
Barrington, 64
Bath Road fire (Newport), 34
Batterson, James G., 133
Bay Queen (boat), 46
Bay View Inn (Jamestown), 95
Beaches, 73, 74, 75, 76, 77, 78, 79, 80, 83
Bedlow, Henry, 33
Bee Hive dress shop (Newport), 153
Bellevue Avenue (Newport), 72, 82
Benedict, David, 124
Benedict, Stephen, 124
Benedict House (Pawtucket), 124
Berkeley, George, 73
Bijou Theatre (Newport), 107
Biltmore Hotel (Providence), 7
Blackstone Canal Bank, 120
Blackstone river, 44
Block Island, 41
Bongartz, J.H., 118
Braman, D.H., 174
Brick Market Square (Newport), 61, 119, 179
Bridges
Briggs, E.A., 28
Broadcast House (Providence), 15
Broad Street (Pawtucket), 62
Broad Street (Providence), 15, 26, 53
Broadway (Newport), 56
Brownell, Emily, 39
Browning, William G., 118
Brown University (Providence), 29, 149
Bucklin, James, 121

Bull House, Henry (Newport), 32
Burnside Statue (Providence), 8
Burrillville, 141
Butler Exchange (Providence), 4, 5
Butts Block Building (Providence), 6

C. Farnum & Co. (Providence), 4
Cadwalader's Arch, Mrs. (Newport), 81
Canal Street (Providence), 127, 168, 172
Canonicus (steamer), 86
Capwell, E.C., 122
Carroll, F.M. and R.F., 122
Carr's Meat and Vegetable Wagon, 148
Casino (Narragansett Pier), 88
Casino (Newport), 82
Cathedral of Saints Peter and Paul
    (Providence), 180
Central Auto Tires (Providence), 6
Central Bridge (Providence), 163, 164, 165, 166
Central Fire Station (Providence), 8, 10
Chace, John B., 151
Charles S. Bush Company, 53
Charles Street (Providence), 172
Chepachet, 54
Child's Harness Shop, 146
Cimarron Construction, 58
City Hall, Providence, 5, 9, 10, 110
City Hotel (Providence), 26
Civil War Monument (Providence), 4, 5, 8, 9, 21
Claiborne Pell Bridge (Newport), 177, 178
Clark Street (Newport), 32
Cliff Villas (Newport), 34
Cliff Walk Hotel (Newport), 34
Cliff Walk (Newport), 55, 81
Clough & Co. (Providence), 147
College Hill (Providence), 16
College Street (Providence), 17
Columbus Celebration (Providence), 114
Connecticut Mutual Life Insurance Co., 120
Constitution Hill (Providence), 31
Continental Steamboat Company, 46
Cove (Providence), 8, 10
Cranston, 36, 65, 156
Crawford Street Bridge (Providence), 170
Crescent Park (East Providence), 102
Cumberland, 134
Curiosity Shop, Bragunn's (Providence), 140

Davisville, 157
Deeley's (Cumberland), 49
Dexter, Ebenezer Knight, 29
Dexter Asylum (Providence), 29
Dexter Street (Pawtucket), 125
Diamond Hill Quarry (Cumberland), 134
Dixon House (Westerly), 52
Dorrance Street (Providence), 6, 15
Doyle, Arthur, 114
Dunkin' Donuts Center (Providence), 63
Dunnell, Henry, 131
Dyer, Charles, 26

Easterbrooks Saddlery (Pawtucket), 146
East Greenwich, 118
Easton's Beach (Newport), 73, 74, 75, 76, 77,
    78, 79, 80.
    see also Newport Beach
East Providence, 50, 102

East Side (Providence), 24, 163, 164, 165, 166
Eddy Street (Providence), 28, 118, 132
Empire Street (Providence), 58
Exchange Place (Providence), 4, 5, 6, 8, 9, 10,
    109.
    see also Kennedy Plaza (Providence)
Exeter, 145

Fales & Jenks Machine Company (Pawtucket), 125
Fall River Line, 47
Fall River & Providence Steamboat Company,
    47
Federal Building (Providence), 12, 13, 21
Fenner House, Arthur (Cranston), 36
Field's Point (Providence), 167
Firestone Auto Supply & Service Store
    (Providence), 63
First Baptist Church (Providence), 20, 24, 98,
    111, 127
First Beach. see Easton's Beach (Newport)
First Congregational Church (Providence), 46
First Light Infantry of Rhode Island, 108
Fishing crew (Newport), 158, 159
Fitz, Levi N., 118
Fleet Bank Building (Providence), 21
Fort Dumplings (Newport), 94
Foster, 109
Fourth National Bank, 120
Fowler Brothers and Fessenden (Providence), 4
French and American Confectionary
    (Providence), 5

Gardner, Ernest, 145
Garnet Street (Providence), 27
Gilbane Co., 20
Glacier Rock (Providence), 103
Glocester, 54
Goddard State Park (Warwick), 47
Goff, A., 175
Gold Medal Creamery (Providence), 139
Gorham Manufacturing Company (Providence),
    20, 127, 128, 129
Great Atlantic & Pacific Tea Co., 179
Greene, "King Richard," 35
Green Pond (Newport), 144

Hall, Prescott, 33
Hall & Lyon Apothecary (Newport), 179
Harrington's Opera House (Providence), 5
Harrison, Peter, 119
Hess and Co., 153
Hillsgrove (Warwick), 66
Hine, Lewis, 126
Holloway's Photo Parlor, 155
Hopelands (Warwick), 35
Hope Valley, 132
Hopkins Coal Pier, 135
Hopkinton, 123
Hospital Trust Building (Providence), 19, 21
Hotel Bristol (Providence), 18
Hotel Dorrance (Providence), 5
H.W. Angell's lumber (Providence), 17

Ida Lewis (steamer), 45
Imperial Theater (Pawtucket), 62
Industrial Bank Tower (Providence), 21, 181
Industrial Trust Company (Providence), 175

INDEX

Infantry Hall (Providence), 105
Interstate 95 construction, 180, 181
Ives, Hope Brown, 35

Jamestown, 65, 95
Jamestown Bridge (Jamestown), 65
Jefferson, Arthur "Jumbo," 149
Jefferson Plain (Providence), 171
Jenks/Jenckes House, Joseph (Pawtucket), 37
Jessop & Sons (Providence), 9
Jewelry factory (Providence), 124
Johnson, Frank, 145

Kaufman's Boston Bakery (Providence), 31
Kennedy Plaza (Providence), 21, 181.
   see also Exchange Place (Providence)
Keystone Company, 124
Kingston, 49
Knight, B.B. and R., 129

La Salle Square (Providence), 63
Law, Ruth, 77
Lees Governor Company (Providence), 9
Leroy Theater (Pawtucket), 62
Lewis, Ida, 45
Libby's Bakery (Newport), 61
Lily Pond (Newport), 70
Linke, Robert B., 151
Long Wharf (Newport), 47

Maine Creamery Company, 52
Main Street (Chepachet), 54
Main Street (Pawtucket), 152
Malbone, Francis, 73
Malbone, Geoffrey, 33
Malbone Place (Newport), 33
Market House (Providence), 16, 18, 19
Market Square (Providence), 17, 18, 19, 110, 168
Martin, Rock, 152
Martin's Garage (Providence), 59
Mason, James B., 26
Matthews Mansion (Newport), 33
McGee, Jack, 77
McKim, Mead & White, 88, 171
Memorial Boulevard (Newport), 34, 55
Memorial Square (Providence), 20.
   see also Post Office Square (Providence)
Merchants National Bank (Providence), 17
Metal Products Corporation Building, 132
Metropolitan French Cleaners & Fancy Dyers (Newport), 143
Metropolitan Rapid Transit Company Bus (Providence), 57
Middletown, 55, 73, 78, 80
Misquamicut (Westerly), 71
Monarch (balloon), 98
Monarch Coffee, 53
Morris's saloon, 154
Mount Hope (steamer), 108
Mt. Pleasant (Providence), 94

Napatree Point (Westerly), 92
Narragansett, 90
Narragansett Bay Oyster Co. (Providence), 138
Narragansett Boat House Club, 164
Narragansett Hotel (Providence), 15

Narragansett Parkway (Warwick), 62
Narragansett Pier, 88, 89
Narragansett Trotting Park, 38
Nasonville, Burrillville, 141
Natick Mills, 129
New Pawtucket Theatre (Pawtucket), 106
Newport, 32, 33, 34, 47, 55, 56, 60, 61, 70, 72, 73, 74, 75, 76, 77, 78, 79, 80, 81, 82, 94, 107, 119, 144, 148, 155, 157, 158, 159, 177, 178, 179
Newport Beach. *see* Easton's Beach (Newport)
Newport Bridge (Newport), 177, 178
Newport harbor, 70
Newport train depot, 51
Newport Waterworks, 155
New Shoreham (steamer), 47
New York, New Haven & Hartford Railroad, 52
Nichols and Langworthy's Machine Shop, 132
North Central State Airport, 67
Northeast Airlines, 67
North Main Street (Pawtucket), 37
North Main Street (Providence), 20, 31, 56, 111, 127

Oakland Beach (Warwick), 83
Ocean House (Newport), 72
Ocean House (Watch Hill), 90
Ockel (clock maker), 131
Old Mill Rller Coaster (Newport), 77
Old Post Road (Apponaug), 63
Olmsted, Frederick Law, 62, 88
Opera House (Providence), 105

Packard, Alpheus Spring, 111
Palmer, James H., 121
Parks and Amusement Parks
Pawtucket, 36, 37, 52, 62, 106, 112, 113, 115, 124, 125, 152
Pawtucket Congregational Church, 44
Pawtuxet river, 65, 176
Pawtuxet River bridge (Cranston), 65
Phenix Bank, 120
Phenix (West Warwick), 122
Point Judith Lighthouse (Narragansett), 91
Point Street Bridge (Providence), 64
Postal Telegraph and Cable Office (Newport), 157
Post Office Bridge (Providence), 12
Post Office Square (Providence), 13
Potowomut Highlands (Warwick), 35
Prospect Terrace (Providence), 24
Providence, 4, 5, 6, 7, 8, 9, 10, 12, 13, 15, 16, 17, 18, 19, 20, 21, 24, 26, 27, 28, 29, 30, 31, 46, 53, 58, 63, 98, 103, 105, 109, 111, 118, 121, 124, 127, 132, 149, 150, 163, 164, 165, 166, 167, 168, 170, 171, 172, 180, 181
Providence City Hall, 5, 9, 10, 16, 110
Providence Civic Center, 63
Providence County Courthouse, 20
Providence harbor, 45
Providence Poor Farm, 29. *see also* Dexter Asylum (Providence)
Providence Public Library, 4, 58
Providence River, 12, 135
Providence Steam and Gas Pipe Company, 15
Providence Washington Insurance Company, 18
Purgatory Chasm (Middletown), 80

Randall brokers (Providence), 17
Red Bridge (Providence), 163, 164, 165, 166
Reeves, David Wallis, 101
Reiner Co. (Providence), 18
Reiner's Druggists (Providence), 6
Rhode Island College, 142
Rhode Island College of Agriculture and Mechanic Arts, 141
Rhode Island Exchange for Woman's Work, 151
Rhode Island Granite Works, 133
Rhode Island Normal School, 142
Rhode Island School of Design (Providence), 19
Richard Borden (steamer), 45
Richmond Saw Mill, 145
Rickard, George A., 28
Ringley's Cafe (Newport), 61
Rivers
   Blackstone River, 44
   Pawtucket River, 65, 176
   Providence River, 12, 135
   Seekonk River, 44, 163, 164, 165, 166
   Warren River, 64
Robert L. Smith and Company, 175
Rocky Hill School (Warwick), 35
Rocky Point Amusement Park (Warwick), 84, 85, 86, 87
Roger Williams Park, 99, 100, 101
Roger Williams Statue (Providence), 24, 25
Roger Williams Statue (Roger Williams Park), 99
Roosevelt Avenue (Pawtucket), 115
Route 1 (Apponaug), 63
Royal Weaving Company (Pawtucket), 126
Ryder Bros. Salt Works, 135

Scituate Reservoir, 176
Seekonk river, 44, 163, 164, 165, 166
Shaw, Edward, 2nd, 131
Ships and boats
   Bay Queen (boat), 46
   Canonicus (steamer), 86
   Ida Lewis (steamer), 45

Ships and boats (cont.)
　　Mount Hope (steamer), 108
　　New Shoreham (steamer), 47
　　Richard Borden (steamer), 45
Shirley, John R., 101
"Silver Pond" (Newport), 70
Silver Spring House (East Providence), 102
Simmons, Franklin, 99
Sisson, Henry, 39
Sisson House, Henry Tillinghast (Little Compton), 39
Sky High Hill (Providence), 103
Slater, Samuel, 112
Smith Hill (Providence), 171, 172
Smithfield Union Bank (Woonsocket), 131
Soldiers and Sailors Monument. see Civil War Monument (Providence)
South Kingston, 49
South Main Street (Providence), 120, 140, 151
South Water Street (Providence), 170
Spencer Block, Phenix, 122
Sprague, A. & W., 38
Sprague House, Amasa (Warwick), 38
Spruce Street (Providence), 30
St. George's School (Middletown), 78
St. John's Masonic Lodge (Providence), 16
Star Theater (Newport), 60
State House (Providence), 171, 172, 173, 181
State Prison (Cranston), 156
Steeple Street (Providence), 127
"Stone Chimney House" (Pawtucket), 36

Stone House Club (Little Compton), 39
Stonington & Providence Railroad, 157
Stott, John, 151
Superior Court House (Providence), 24

Tallman, Wiliam, 121
Tanner Street (Newport), 148
T.F. Green Airport (Warwick), 66
Thames Street (Newport), 60, 73, 157, 179
Thomas Pearce City Coal Yard (Providence), 45
Times Square (Pawtucket), 52
Tockwotten House (Providence), 26
Toole, William K., 152
Tribune Building (Providence), 175
Tudor, Frederick, 144
Turk's Head Building (Providence), 175
Turk's Head neighborhood (Providence), 174

Union Bank (Providence), 17
Union Passenger Depot (Providence), 9, 10, 11, 98, 168
Union Railroad Depot (Providence), 18, 54
Union Railroad trolleys (Providence), 53
Union Railway Company (Providence), 17
Union Station (Providence), 14, 21
Unitarian Church (Providence), 46
University of Rhode Island, 141
U.S. Hotel (Newport), 73

Vanity Fair Amusement Park (East Providence), 102

Vartan Gregorian School (Providence), 26
Vernon House (Newport), 32
Waldorf Lunch (Providence), 130
Warren, 107, 146
Warren, Russell, 121
Warren river, 64
War stamps, selling, 110
Warwick, 35, 38, 47, 62, 63, 66, 83, 84, 85, 86, 87, 122
Warwick Downs, 62
Washington Buildings (Providence), 18, 168
Washington Street (Providence), 6, 7, 58
Watchemoket Square (East Providence), 50
Watch Hill (Westerly), 91, 92, 93
Waterman Street (Providence), 163
Westerly, 52, 71, 91, 92, 93, 133
Westminster Street (Providence), 114, 118, 121, 130, 131, 151, 174
Weybosset Bridge (Providence), 168, 169, 170
Weybosset Street (Providence), 17, 19, 26, 53, 168, 169, 170, 174
What Cheer Building (Providence), 120
What Cheer Cottage (Roger Williams Park), 99
White Co., A.A., 175
Whitman, Jacob, 174
Williams, Betsey, 99
Williams, Joshua Appleby, 32, 70
Winslow, William, 87
World War I Memorial (Providence), 20
W.W. Whipple Company (Providence), 139

Young's Gift Shop (Providence), 150

PHOTO CREDITS

Brown University Library: 127, 128a/b, 129

Collection of the Author: 8a, 90, 101b, 154a/b

Collection of William J. Connors: 4, 5a, 17, 28b, 29a, 32a, 32b, 33a/b, 34a, 36a/b, 41a, 45a/b, 46a/b, 49a, 52b, 54a, 64a/b, 70a/b, 72a/b, 73a/b, 74a, 80b, 81b, 83a/b, 84a/b, 85a/b, 86a/b, 89, 91a, 91b, 94a, 98 a/b, 99a/b, 100a, 101a, 102b, 105a, 107b, 111, 118b, 120, 121a/b, 123a/b, 124a/b, 132a, 133a/b, 134, 141a, 146a, 147b, 148a, 149.

Collection of Lawrence R. DePetrillo: 6, 7, 11, 12, 14, 18a, 19, 20, 26b, 41b, 63b, 74b, 100b, 109a/b, 110a/b, 114, 122, 131a, 163, 164a, 165a/b, 167a/b, 168, 169, 170, 176a/b, 180b

Library of Congress: 108, 126, 129b

Collection Matthew R. Isenburg: 174a

Collection of the Newport Historical Society: 34b, 47a, 55, 56b, 61, 65b, 77, 80a, 81b, 82a/b, 95, 119, 144, 147a, 153, 158, 159, 179a

Courtesy of the Pawtucket Public Library: 37, 44, 52a, 59, 62b, 106, 112, 113a/b, 115, 125, 146b, 152

Providence Public Library: 15a, 27, 29b, 30, 38, 39, 40, 48a, 50, 51, 57, 60, 66, 67, 75, 76, 79, 88, 102a, 103, 105b, 107, 113a/b, 138, 139, 140, 141b, 142, 143, 148b, 150, 155, 156, 157a/b, 166, 171a/b, 172b, 174b, 175b, 178, 179b

Providence Warwick CVB: 21, 25

Rhode Island State Archives: 4,5, 8b, 10, 13, 15b, 16, 18b, 24, 26a, 28a, 31, 35, 47b, 49b, 53, 54b, 56a, 58, 62a, 63a, 65a, 71, 78, 87, 92, 93, 104, 118a, 130b, 135, 145, 151a/b, 164b, 172a, 175a, 177a/b, 180a, 181a/b